Published by Bloomberg Publishing., Dover, Delaware

Interior Design by Mayra González

ISBN 978-1-7363410-0-1

Printed in the United States of America

DEDICATION 5

PREFACE 7

SECTION I: THE BEGINNING. 11

CHAPTER 1: Why Me? 13
CHAPTER 2: Listen to Your Elders 19
CHAPTER 3: Anything You Want to Learn You Can Self-Teach Yourself. The Library Has Endless Knowledge. 31
CHAPTER 4: If They Are Not Masters of the Advice You Are Looking For, Find the Masters. Do Not Listen to Anyone Not Doing What You Want to Do. 35
CHAPTER 5: It is Difficult to Be a King In Your Own Backyard. 41
CHAPTER 6: If It Were Easy, Everyone Would Be Doing It 45
CHAPTER 7: Emotions Are a Luxury We Cannot Afford. 51

SECTION II: CHANGING MINDSET AND PRIORITIES 61

CHAPTER 8: Why Should it Be Lonely at the Top? 63
CHAPTER 9: Collected Realities to the Fundamentals of Wealth Creation 67
CHAPTER 10: Unmeasured Time is Lost Time 71
CHAPTER 11: Reset, Refocus, Recommit 75
CHAPTER 12: RRR In Everyday Life-RRR247 79
CHAPTER 13: You Cannot Reset the Past, Move Forward 81
CHAPTER 14: Golden Rule is Golden Life 83
CHAPTER 15: The Power of Multiple Streams of Income 87

SECTION III: ENGINEERING AN INCREDIBLE FUTURE FOR ALL 97

CHAPTER 16: The Changing World and What It Means to You 99
CHAPTER 17: The Family Economy 103
CHAPTER 18: When the Family Economy Takes on Systems of Free Enterprise 109
CHAPTER 19: Benefitting From a Family of "Family Economies" All Using "System of Free Enterprise". 111
CHAPTER 20: Community Strength in Numbers 113
CHAPTER 21: The Blessing of Paying it Forward 119
CHAPTER 22: Take Action. Where to Begin. 123

SECTION IV: RORY'S MARKETING 101 CLASS BEGINS HERE 127

CHAPTER 23: Ascension Marketing and The Patient Process 129

CHAPTER 24: Coca-Cola Marketing 135

CHAPTER 25: Indirect Marketing 139

CHAPTER 26: Lures and Attraction Marketing 141

CHAPTER 27: Cross Marketing 145

SECTION V: RORY'S APPLIED MARKETING 101 CLASS BEGINS HERE 149

CHAPTER 28: Content Marketing 151

CHAPTER 29: Social Media Marketing Through the Eyes of Rory 153

CHAPTER 30: Link Posting, Online Ads, and The Power of Numbers 157

CHAPTER 31: Three-Legged Marketing Table 159

SECTION VI: THE GLOBAL VISION. MAKING THE WORLD AMAZING. 163

CHAPTER 32: The New Way of Working Together 165

CHAPTER 33: Core Values 167

CHAPTER 34: Applying Core Values in Everyday Life 169

CHAPTER 35: Applying Core Values in Building an Online Marketing Community 171

CHAPTER 36: End with a Never - Ending Path. An Introduction to the Performance Blogging System (PBS). 173

CHAPTER 37: An Encore of Gratitude 177

DEDICATION

This book is dedicated to my wife, Tanya, my sons' Gaven, Garet, Edison, Graysen, Tytan, and Ryver. To my daughters' Wynter, Breale, and Chloe. My grandson Malak and my granddaughter Ava. And to the entire RRR247 Family to which we are in proud service to be "Always Growing" with. And of course, to my mother, Trell, who brought me into this world and thankfully put me in an environment to grow and never dousing my drive, ambition, and goals.

The work I do every day I do for God, family, free enterprise, and an effort to better humanity. I truly strive to help humanity by sharing with everyone and being willing and teachable. I am here to make a difference--one of legacy. This legacy I dedicate to the memory of my grandfather, Richard Merlin Thorup. I know he is looking down on me with incredible pride. I do this in his honor and am forever grateful to have had him in my life. I love you so much Grandpa.

I have been blessed in incredible ways and am thankful to so many people. I am a huge believer in Christ and am entirely thankful to GOD for whom absolute patience, understanding, and unconditional love, are forever cherished by me. I live a life of freedom. This very life is made possible from the many things I am sharing here. Marketing is the overall sum of what I do best. I have always understood marketing and how it works. I see the world through the eyes of an "all the time marketer." It is not a view shared by all. Though it is a view that allows for incredible success in all aspects of life and is why I am writing this book. To understand marketing, is to understand all that it takes to create understanding, happiness, and wealth. With wealth and knowledge comes freedom. And with freedom we can all truly be at our best.

There are some incredible tools to teach and share this vision. For me, if there was a product to encompass the soul of marketing, it would be fine wines. And as you enjoy the journey this book will take you on, you now have a way to enjoy it. You cannot eat this book and you cannot rip a piece of marketing to eat. You can, however, take a bottle of fine wine, pour it into a nice crystal wine glass and press it to your lips. Allow the elixir of years of love and labor to pour over your lips and to be consumed and enjoyed.

My life and success have led me to a path of fine wines. Not just as a product to share in the best manner and value possible, but for what it represents to our lives. The path of wine and everything Incredible with it, I dedicate to Jim Rohn. The reason for all paths leading to wine began with Jim and I enjoying the first of timely meals and celebration that would shape my life forever. He was a great man and a true inspiration for me in many ways. I give thanks for the time he spent with me when he did and for the path it created in my life and the lives of all those I can share it with. He was all about marketing and all about freedom. And Jim loved fine wine. I know we are onto something and to share it is only the right thing to do.

And while we are going through some great things in the pages to come, I suggest a pairing of a fine Ricord Merlot or an inspirational glass of More Than Muse Cabernet Sauvignon to aid in the absorption of the words within. This will allow you to take this knowledge in and celebrate it with every drop of wine as we go forward.

PREFACE

My life's work, as revealed in the teachings and instructions within these pages, however, are dedicated to Richard Merlin Thorup, my grandfather and role model to which I built the structure of the man I became today. There is truly a need for a father in our lives and in my case, a grandfather. I would also add to my mentors as I grew, I gained a road to knowledge in what has become a thriving career through the doorway given to by one Richard C. Davidson. To whom a 14-year-old Rory Ricord went from college and lawyer bound to feeding his entrepreneur spirit and hunger in a fearless mindset to constantly get up when knocked down.

Because mentors mean so much to who I am today and to where this journey of life continues to go, I feel there are a few to which mentioning just feels right. They may not have realized that their care and selflessness with a persistent and passion driven, energetic young man would grow to help so many others. They were stones into the foundation of what has become. To every soul touched by the ripple effect of everything shared within these pages; gratitude for all of it coming together in the manner to which it has.

As for the wine, it was adding wine and the aspects of wine that changed everything. In everything I have done, continue to do and to that which I look forward to doing, Wine is always there. Whether it be indirectly, subtly, or as direct as a beaming ray of sunshine first thing in the morning. Oddly enough, it is referenced in the Bible 231 times either indirectly, subtly, or as direct as a beaming ray of sunshine first thing in the morning. And like anything great, the unfolding of this will occur as you venture through the pages within. These are all my words and unedited by others as I let the experience and weight of everything I wanted to share be expressed by and through me and the inspirations around me. Jim Rohn and his teachings are responsible for setting me on the road of wine and understanding what wine truly is. Wine is celebration and it truly sums up the emotions and struggles along the way to success.

Like a true fine wine, we are going to begin, grow and develop and then finish off to something wonderful. I have had a blessed life with some incredible mentors. They are the minerals from which the fruits of my knowledge and creations have been developed. The environment of learning and growth that was affected by each of my mentors is the collective understanding and "fruit" that I have the privilege to share with you here.

The knowledge I am sharing is a path not only for wealth in money, but wealth in all areas of your life. Balance is key and fundamental for true success. You can excel in any one area of life and at the cost of others. True happiness is found when you have balance. You then share in the abundance or as I want to enlighten everyone with, the overabundance of everything good. To me, this is the true meaning of life here on earth. And like a true fine wine, it can be enjoyed best by those that are seeking the experience of the product of growth, experience, and success like that of a fine wine.

I am going to use the power of the written word to enrich the fruit of knowledge contained within these pages. May they enrich and grow your understanding. I heard many of the lessons I am sharing here over the years. Some of them were easy to understand and some came with experience. Then some I thought I understood but it was not until later in life I fully began to understand.

May you gain knowledge and as you read this again and again, even after months and years of growth; may it continue to share and pay the knowledge forward.

So, enjoy a glass of Ricord Merlot along the Journey you are about to share. If I had it my way, we would be discussing this along a coastal setting. One with mountains behind us and the ocean in front of us. So, imagine if you would that we are in a place such as that and let us begin.

SECTION I

THE BEGINNING

CHAPTER 1

WHY ME?

Before anything can be set into motion, the "WHY" or reason for the purpose to set it in motion is best to realize and understand. The sheer act of picking up this book and reading it was done out of a "Why". This is not a mere story of fiction. And it is not intended for just entertainment. Its purpose is to share and pay forward knowledge and understanding that took the years of an overachiever, an anomaly socially and a person of grit to understand and then be able to share with others. When it comes to getting ready to change your Mindset and Priorities, I find it best to analyze where you are now. For your understanding and identification of things to change, you need to realize where you are starting from. See it is pretty much certain that you represent the same actions and directions of your environment. With today's technologies and the incredible access that is ever growing online, the ability to open and change your environment has truly never been this accessible. The moment you opened this book, you allowed change to influence and happen in your life. Congratulations and know that I am smiling in delight that you are allowing my discoveries to enlighten and bless your life as they have mine. Let us begin with Environment shall we.

For instance, if you grew up with parents that were employees, odds are you are an employee. If you grew up with parents who were business owners, odds are you are a business owner. This continues in most things: how we think, what we do for fun, and how we spend our precious 24 hours of each day. We are typically a combination of the environment around us. I figure we are 90% of the environment we are raised in. And this has its own boundaries. We may be comfortable in our environment. Though taking from some key things I have discovered, this is not the case for those of us that realize we are meant to have more.

For Christians, it is taught that it is as simple as turning to Christ. And as easy as that sounds it comes with an entire instruction manual known as the Bible. Stay tuned, you are about to gain lifetimes of knowledge to allow you a better and happier life. And may it parallel the teachings of Christ in modern day verbiage. I have always considered Christ a mentor and path to follow.

Once you achieve some balance in all areas of life, get ready to be a beacon of hope and possibility for others. That is how this all works. We Pay It Forward. I am excited about what the future holds. I am also excited about your future.

There is a pattern to this that affects us all. And unless we turn to changing our environment, we are set to follow the environment we know. For we do not know what we don't know. And if what we do know is not making our dreams, goals and creating the ability to help others, then it is time for you to expand on your environment.

See, I see it pretty clear. Poverty and the outcomes of poverty will only continue. The poor will always remain poor unless they rise up and change their environment (and the teachings and patterns of that new environment). The same can be said for the middle class and upper middle class. And if you are keeping up, I am literally about to explain and offer you the secret to wealth.

Though unlike what you may be expecting, this is not just about you. See, the secret to wealth that I discovered is not in being that 1% of 1% that make it to multiple hundreds of millions or billions while others just miss out. It is about gaining wealth, being able to pass that wealth on long after you leave this world and do it in a way that spreads the wealth to several others all at the same time.

If you want to become wealthy in money and time, then keep reading because I figured it out and figured out how to share it with literally anyone willing to change their environment. This is not just about how "YOU" can become rich; it is about how you can help change the wealth of so many others. We get to attack poverty and offer a real-world solution to enhance the lives and lifestyles of so many. This is a movement. This is a shift that defies the voices of Mainstream Media and global-controlled thinking. This is not about the few but the many.

Truth and logic should always be felt and heard. When you operate out of truth, logic is easy to explain. When you operate from truth, things are just easier. It is when mistruth's, corrupted truths, exaggerated truths or any other form of a lie that things become complicated. Truths are simple.

My Grandfather was a solid fixture in my life. From the time I was five we were living four minutes by bicycle from him. Just a couple of subdivisions (neighborhoods) away. My path in life was then forged by the environment created by those around and influencing my life on a daily basis. Even the "not so good" influences set the environmental learning into motion.

Environment learning for me was where I heeded the advice of "listen to your elders". From there, it was, "anything you want to learn you can self-teach yourself. The Library has endless knowledge." Then it was, "if they are not masters of the advice you are looking for, find the masters. Do not listen to anyone not doing what you want to do." Then this Gem that has been proven true countless times: "you cannot be a King in your own backyard." A fun one that usually comes up when a project or learning curve is met head on is: "If it were easy, everyone would be doing it." And finally, a powerful environmental learning principal: "emotions are a luxury we cannot afford."

"Listen to your elders," history unknown, is sure to repeat itself. There is absolutely no shame in learning from others. And those that take the knowledge are sure to gain an edge and hand up towards their own progress.

"Anything you want to learn you can self-teach yourself. The Library has endless knowledge." Thankful every day for my Grandpa Thorup setting me on this course of thought. Looking and seeking knowledge. We have the tools and information at our fingertips. And we can access unlimited information today from one of hundreds of devices all connected to the information.

"If they are not masters of the advice you are looking for, find the masters. Do not listen to anyone not doing what you want to do." This can be the most logical yet unrecognized freedom we all have. The ability to appreciate the advice of those around us, but to seek the proper advice from those that really know and understand.

"It is difficult to be a King in your own backyard." This saying I heard at a young age. It was at a sales training I attended when I was 12. I was listening to gentlemen that seemed to have the lifestyle I wanted for my family. It made sense and I went on to really utilize it. Especially with regards to creating and sharing success with others.

"If it were Easy, everyone would be doing it." One of my favorite lessons in life. Heard many times in the circles of business owners, entrepreneurs, and creators. It is a common road of perception when working through issues, solving problems, and creating something better than what you had or knew of before. It is both an explanation for how some gain more than others and how some help others so that all can gain more.

"Emotions are a luxury we cannot afford." This was taught to me by Jack Hinman, who for several years was the CTO of my Lead Generation and Training and Systems Technology Company. It was passed on training to him by a mentor in his life and I am continuing to pass it down here to you. This principal alone has saved me in so much unnecessary harm to my mental self, my financial self and has been more of a turning point in wisdom. If you look at anything in life, decisions in life, or points in your life where things seemed to take a fork in the wrong direction, this is where you are about to be given an understanding and a gift to change your life for the better.

Now that you have a simple direction with those environmental learning principles, let us spend a chapter on each one. This is where your mind should be opening up. More so, you are going to be going through a process allowing for growth. And I might add, this is for all areas of life.

Also, when it comes to the "Why Me" of it all; while I am a product of several learning philosophies and understandings; I want to share my knowledge forward. Whatever you think you understand about marketing and the persuasion and attention gaining methods used to help people make Decisions, this very book will enhance your abilities and understanding.

CHAPTER 2

LISTEN TO YOUR ELDERS.

This was not a difficult one for me. But I have seen it be a difficult action for others to understand. Respect for our elders allows us to gain from another person's lifetime. This is an environmental blessing for seriously everyone. If you can take the time to hear stories and life lessons from others, especially your elders, you are truly investing in your future. And it does not have to come from your direct environment. From picking up this book, to opening up your comprehension and awareness, you can allow Elders around you to share with you. And they absolutely love doing so. You will see a sparkle come into their eyes and they will just share away. Humanity is history being shared to improve upon itself for the future. In the family unit, there is power when one generation truly works to enhance and benefit the next. Therefore, the evildoers of the world have been attacking the family unit. It allows for the betterment of the next generation. It allows the natural progression of everything to occur. We naturally want to create a better life and better future for our children than what we had ourselves.

I was born the first grandson on both sides of my family. Born to the oldest of both sides of the family. Both my mother's side and father's side, the siblings to my parents, were more like older siblings to me than aunts or uncles. This was my environment. And it was one that was beneficial for me. I had a young grandmother on my father's side, My Grandfather to whom my middle name was passed on through was recently deceased prior to my arrival to this awesome planet. Also, I might add being born to a Mormon-based religious belief system (or as preferred politically now Latter-Day Saints) in the self-sufficient state of Utah, in the best country ever known, America.

I was encouraged and supported in my entrepreneurial ways from a young age. From eight years old, sales and marketing were my thing. I was born with a silver tongue and somehow understood early on that listening and asking the right questions would get me what I wanted. While I did not come from a Silver Spoon (far from it), I desired more for my siblings, myself, and my mother. These were driving factors that set me off on the ways of finding my path and to be led to the time and financial freedoms of what marketing can create.

My father was always best when in the Military. He was a Marine and had left the service sometime after Vietnam and his marrying my mother. He wished to be full-time Military and after failed jobs and businesses he returned to the structure and known environment of the Military. Only he went to the Army as it was best suited to stay in Utah where mom wanted to be. That kept me with my Grandpa and that was a great thing for me.

My father contributed to my environment and path to where I am today. In 1984, the monopoly of telephones with "Mother Bell" occurred. A once-controlled utility, the phone company used to be one company. You had to lease the phone even. When this transition occurred, my father took his military background in teletypewriters and military communications to form Telephone Service and Supply. To which I listened, learned, and even participated in doing and learning the trade. Unknown to me at the time, it was allowing me the knowledge to change my direction in life towards my goals, dreams, and desires.

In the 80's, it was about buying something in bulk and selling it individually for me; I represented various Companies in door-to-door sales. And really learned the art of conversation, building rapport and trust. From there, it was about presentation and interest. Mason Shoes, American Greeting Cards and so many other items that I could sell to my surrounding neighbors. My Grandfather set me up with Mason Shoes. He liked them and agreed to be my first customer. Explaining the selling points and introducing me to a sales manual that was provided by the company, I devoured it and applied its teachings. I did not know what I did not know, and I was soaking up everything.

My mother was a professional Commercial Artist. She was trained and had an incredible eye for the work she did. She hand drew diesel trucks, tractors, motorcycles, and such to then be placed on ball caps, t-shirts, and printed materials of every kind. She was working for printing shops and was busy all the time. She had a niche, solid clientele, and constant work. Though it was based on the labor she alone did and allowed her to be home for us when we came home from school, it was not exactly raking in the profits. Watching my parents struggle drove my desire to change things for me.

My mother would take me to the printers she worked with and I found another product to sell. Since my mother was doing the art and had moved to computers, I was already understanding programs allowed for set up and design. I also found great pride in my mother's work for various art pieces that were popular for people to put on the walls in their homes. I sold art door to door and then ventured into "mom and pop" restaurants and shops to sell business cards, menus, ad flyers and whatever else they needed.

I was building up a clientele and was making more in the marketing and sales side of printing than the art and labor side of the work being done. This led me to look for a Mentor and to listen to those that had been in that career-space for years. One printing broker was an incredible support for me from the time I was 14. This was Richard Davidson. He had a client in computer telephony. And one day while we were at the same printing shop, Richard with his computer telephony client, and me with various clients work in progress. During our conversation together I saw a user manual for his computer telephony client. I asked if I could look at it. I read it and was instantly interested in selling the technology. The technology was Voice Messaging. The service was adding a toll-free number to the Voice Messaging so small businesses could look and act like a large business.

Within a couple weeks, Richard had something better for me. His company had an internal office support center. It was the mailroom-slash-sales support. It did not pay much but I could be around the technology from the inside and learn it. I wanted an additional income stream. I was soon needing my own car, as I was about to be the legal age to drive. I took the opportunity and ran with it. This led to learning the technology and with my background in telephones and building cables and working with Commercial Phone Systems. I quickly adapted to the large phone switches and understanding to run things. Because there were other needs in the business and no one else seemed to be stepping up, I went to work.

Soon I had built up a collections process for the company. I figured out ways to improve our billing and collecting. And figured out different ways to create additional products and services within the computer system that we were using. I studied and tested different ideas and possibilities. I learned and adapted the voice messaging computers and software to service the needs of customers.

Richard was always checking in and we talked over things many times. He was more than helpful, and his best advice was what he both told me and showed me. He was a Navy man. He was someone that literally jumped from a helicopter, then dove down and planted explosives. He also was a much-needed father figure and solid shoulder of reason for a determined youth.

Richard knew and supported me in anything I wanted to do. He would always tell me I had something special and was proud to be my friend. The best advice he gave me though was to make it happen, do my best, and to listen and learn. In the years of watching him, he would listen and take things in. I got it. And that allowed me to make things happen in a big way.

To this day, Richard shares ideas and directions. His sharing of his experiences in life, marriage, kids, careers, and passions have been guidance for me for over three decades now. From the moment he saw my interest in voice messaging, he did everything he could to get me involved. He put forth incredible efforts and sacrificed time, driving, and even loaned me his car to help me get things set up. He was there for me all through the beginning and checked-in ongoing. He also introduced me to the concept of enjoying a hand spun shake and the value of always having a crisp hundred-dollar bill in your wallet. Not to spend it, but to have when it all seems down and gloomy, "Hey you have one hundred dollars, and you can always make it grow!"

Richard was formally educated as well as years of service in the Navy. Yet he supported me in decisions that were greatly directional for me. Before the voice messaging interest and passionate knowledge, I was seeking in that field, I was college bound. More so, being raised by a "proud marine", I had been raised in a military manner and have a footlocker that I cannot get rid of to this day. Because I was determined to be a millionaire, I was set to be an attorney from a young age. It was understanding statistics, math and being true to me and thankfully Richard was there to help set me straight. I had worked on the knowledge, worked on the grades and West Point was in my sites. My father would have been proud, and I would have been miserable. That realization, and the realization that though they probably mean well, people that are giving advice on something they know nothing about, should stay out of things they do not know. Something so important I dedicated an entire chapter to the topic.

I had teachers at the college I was taking classes at during my last years of high school tell me my way of marketing and sales was wrong. Questioning everything and seeking answers from those doing what I wanted to be doing, I ended my college and university directions. Life was teaching me as I went and clearly college or university was not in-line with what was best for me. Definitely not right for what I wanted to get out of life.

Plus, I should add that I had multiple streams of income already and my marketing and sales understanding were working well on them all, so seeing that the advice of the college professors gave was incorrect was plain to see. I say to listen to your elders, but it is taking from it what you should that matters. Not all things are correct for you. And sometimes it is realizing you have it right even when you are told it is wrong. Especially where technology and innovations in how we communicate are involved. It was evolving back then and continues to today.

As I was building and networking, I was also learning the way of trends. Other products and services that were going the same direction I was already heading. Somehow, the way I was marketing and selling was not only working with the main products I had chosen to market, but with multiple products in addition. I still laugh at the fact I had multiple teachers tell me that what I was doing was wrong. Sales and marketing are clearly diverse. Marketing makes the world go around. And when marketing is done right; sales becomes order taking. Something that clearly was good to understand for mail order and especially online.

There is a lot to be said for those that cannot do something, they often teach that very something. My methods, my way of seeing things, was clearly not the status quo. That and I was consuming knowledge and keeping up with the new directions that were being created. And at a time when computers and their use and availability to the masses was exploding.

I had discovered that it was understanding people that was the real professional path I was on. The products or services I was marketing and selling were secondary. This we will cover throughout the book. Just realize the methods to marketing and then sales that I live by are useful no matter the product or service you are representing. Literally the products and services are completely secondary to the understanding of the people to whom you are marketing to.

Before I was 17, I was travelling all over the US doing sales presentations and training. I was balancing the rest of my high school education. Because of my understanding and skill sets with computers, computer telephony and ability to sell and market already I was in a great place. Luckily for me, I was the only competent computer user in the building. So, I was involved in the meetings, taking copious notes, and involved in all aspects. I just made it happen. Shortly after graduating high school, I took over the International Marketing Director position. My decisions were increasing in my compensation and wealth and taking me around the globe. We were operating in 12 Countries and I was running staff in 3 offices and was travelling all through the US, Canada, Europe, United Kingdom, Asia, and Australia.

This led to a path of discovery and enjoyment of fine wines. It began at the age of 22. It was in Germany at the conclusion of yet another European Extravaganza Event. While enjoying the after-event staff dinner, Jim Rohn had requested to eat with me alone at a table away from the rest of the staff. I was beyond honored and I had also put it out to the Universe that this evening I would get some alone time with Jim. Like I had discovered years before, asking for things in the right way, with gratitude and the knowledge it was deserved was a sure way to see that it would happen. This evening was a great start. I know we began the Dinner with a Cocktail. Though for the life of me, that detail as to what the cocktail was has escaped my mind completely. I was into dirty martini's (still am on the right occasion) but cannot fully remember. I can however remember the very details of the evening from the time Jim and I sat down and began to order our meal.

Jim and I were looking at the menu and the staff had already secured the entirety of the restaurant for us. The wait staff was in full show and very attentive. There was no spared expense, and we were all accustomed to this treatment after such events. I decided on the Filet Mignon, which Jim also chose. Medium rare and with a salad to begin. I had blue cheese and Jim went with a vinaigrette. After ordering the Filet Mignon, Jim asked for the wine menu and asked me if I would like to share a bottle of wine. I said sure; to which he immediately asked what sounded good. I really had no clue at this time in my life. Being well versed on liquor and spirits (as much as three solid years of first-class travel would afford), I was not a big fan of wine. Not because of taste, but because of ignorance. No one I was around while growing up really drank wine. I was raised religious in a manner that did not allow for alcohol of any type; I had not consumed a drop of alcohol until I was 18 ½ years old. And after I had moved out on my own. So, my response was a blank look.

I had not really paid attention to wine. I knew of some and other than knowing red was a choice for red meat; I was far from ready for this question. I replied with why don't you pick something. It was obvious that I was not a wine person. Jim, as he would, began to teach me many of his teachings beginning with wine. Jim selected and verbally stated we would be having a Cabernet Sauvignon from the menu. He then signaled for the wait staff that was attentively standing by. He smiled upon selecting it and said, "Oh we deserve this." I smiled back, not knowing what he was referencing. The server was right on it. Within a few minutes, the server returned with the selected bottle in hand and presented it to Jim. Jim showed it to me, and I noticed it was from Napa Valley, California. Jim responded to the waiter with a great big smile and requested it to be decanted. The server took the bottle and went back into the kitchen. For the longest time, as I recalled this story, I would always laugh that we went all the way to Germany to enjoy a bottle of wine from California. Back then it was hilarious to me. Today, however, it could not mean more to me.

As the waiter was seeing to the decanting; the conversation unfolding was about to change my life. I say this in regard to several things. This meal was an event for me. It set me on a road. And this road not only led to wine, but started many roads, all of which connected to wine at the end of it all.

Keep reading, the road is not short, and you should be on a second glass of Ricord Merlot by now anyway. And know that I am smiling big as you share this incredible moment in my life with me. There are pivotal times in our life. Reflecting on them and seeing where things changed is important. For me, this single experience with Jim Rohn was super pivotal. I cannot wait until we meet once again. While in his lifetime, he became a legend. He has helped so many to see things in a better light. I am honored to be passing his timeless teachings and honoring him by living to the best of what he taught me every day.

We were in Germany and Jim went on to explain that there were incredible wines all around the globe and how even in Germany, which was known for its beer, had an incredible heritage in wines. He also broke down some knowledge on the different varietals of wine. I made a comment that I did not understand why some wine was $7 and wines in the restaurants were so much more. I was curious as to why people would spend so much for a beverage. It was something I was curious about. Up to this point, I had had wines on the plane in first class and had not really understood much other than I liked the way it made me feel.

The salads arrived and we had finished our cocktails. The wine followed in a decanter. It was the first time I had seen a decanter up close. It was also clear as to how I reacted that I was seeing this device for the first time. Jim explained how it opened up the wine to let it breathe. The waiter poured Jim's glass with about 2 ounces. Jim looked at the wine in the Glass, smiled. Then Jim smelled the Wine, smiled. He swirled his glass on the table making it whirl around. And then he sipped and savored. He swallowed and said, "delicious." To which the waiter poured my glass halfway and then poured more into Jim's glass setting both the bottle and the decanter next to us on the table.

It was then that I asked Jim why he chose a California wine when we were in Germany. He chuckled somewhat and explained that it was a really good wine. And that some of the best wines are from Napa Valley and the surrounding areas. Jim went on to discuss the manner to which Wine was produced and what really goes into each bottle of fine wine. I had never been to a winery before. However, I had made wine with a close friend that I met while making beer. I discussed beer making and my experience in making a blueberry wine. I remember because when Jim broke down the Wine making process and the process to making beer, I realized I understood more than I thought I did. I also realized the costs of the raw materials and things began to make more and more sense.

We discussed a lot during the dinner. We moved through the Salad and enjoyed the wine with our Filet Mignon. We moved to cappuccino and some chocolate cake that was being had by all the staff and then Jim suggested we get some Port. Now, I had seen port in the Duty-Free Shops and since everything was going perfectly, I agreed. It was Tawny Port; he had chosen it from the wine menu, and we enjoyed that, and it was time to leave the restaurant. We had been discussing the importance of taking time to enjoy life and reflect. The Europeans did things right. Long dinners and conversation. Sometimes two or three hours long. We were anything but rushed. The comparison of the way we were treated as compared to the United States was pointed out to me. And after an incredible 3 hour dinner and life changing conversation, Jim and I were not done that evening.

We moved on from the restaurant and headed to the bar for cigars and scotch. I was in heaven. I knew scotch better than wine and by now my education on the value and location of Wines and spirits was becoming exciting. Passionate would be the answer. For as we enjoyed the cigar and scotch and Jim retired; I knew I had some incredible perspective. And my love for fine food was now combined with fine wine. My favorite meals would now be events and taking time to celebrate and enjoy the company became something to "slow down" for me. This was all because Jim and I were able to converse and he was able to share incredible knowledge and understanding.

I am going to share something that has been a complete part of all my success. The learning and understanding of those that came before us. When I reflect on the shared struggles and successes from my elders it was clear they learned and prospered forward from the generations before them. And this was something I saw great value in, especially if I wanted to get further in life faster than those who came before me.

And while I had respect for Jim Rohn as a speaker, the learned knowledge and methods shared to enjoy my time and to "slow down" and to enjoy an event in a long meal with great food, great wine and great company was priceless. It set me up for several things that have truly benefited me all these years. It also set me into studying and consuming wines everywhere I travelled. I began making Wineries part of my travelling agendas wherever I was able too. I will also add that if you ever want to see a great presentation on marketing; visit the tasting rooms of any Winery. Or attend a virtual tasting in todays, "online wonderland connecting a few to several Thousands of us in a shared virtual event". The marketing process is one to behold.

From experiences of products and services to the types of Women to date, I can tell you that the areas of importance to listen to are not always what you think are important at the time. If you can ever record to paper (writing it down), video (recording it), you can surely use it time and time again. Sometimes it will take a few repeat "Listens" or "Views" to allow it to fully sink into your learning and actions in the future. Sometimes it is a mere "I told you so" when you reflect on the shared knowledge after you made the choice to learn the lesson the hard way. Sometimes suffering through a bad decision on your own is necessary to appreciate the next lesson. And some of us are just slow learners.

I like to think that I live by my own advice today. Advice that is a passing of knowledge and experiences both my own and those shared with me by my Elders. The lessons I have learned came with time, patience, and several failures. Successes were and always will be great and I celebrate them with huge smiles, great wine and the best of Company. Never Alone. Success is the applied lessons and understandings from the failures before it. Hopefully lessons not all learned by you but shared from your Elders and Mentors before you. Listening to the failures (and not just the successes) of others is incredible. Even in the construct of this very book I turned to my Elders and Mentors. I have written thousands of blog pages and marketing pieces. But never have I written out an entire book. Nor have I gone the publishing route.

Thankfully, I am not a starving artist and I have great Mentors, Elders in almost every case. They have guided me through this accomplishment. Though to bring to light, that it is not one, or a few that deserve Credit for sharing with me all these years. I have been blessed with several Mentors. Many to which I sought out and many that the Universe put us into paths to collide and touch each other's life. I have mentioned a few in this book and believe me, several deserve some reflection. One Mentor in particular needs to be thanked with huge gratitude. Universal timing was perfect and that tells me that incredible things are happening.

And while a reference to him would normally belong in the Preface of this book; it is here within this very Chapter that it is most deserved. So, thank you Kosta Gara for your mentorship of over 17 years and for your shared Vision and Understanding as we make this World a better place. This book would never have been the masterpiece it is had you not shared the priceless details and knowledge as you did so freely to me my friend, My brother. I cannot wait to share another bottle (or 3) with you again and again. Some incredible things happened because of you before as they will again. As we reflect on years past, some are hilarious as they worked out. Grateful our paths merged. It is also a note that in gratitude, some that is so special to me I can only let you know that the Kosta Gara wines are a mere token of gratitude. I highly recommend a glass for celebration of something Wonderful.

The Universe works in mysterious ways. And your Elders have messages that are timeless if you but listen to them. You can learn a lot from spending a Saturday afternoon with them even. Take them to lunch and if you want to really enjoy the time, take them somewhere they should enjoy that is a new experience for them. The price of a meal can be well spent. And it is the "Right Energy". You are giving to receive. You can gain the same with a bottle of Wine or a Particular Spirit they enjoy.

From there just get to know what they did to get where they got too. The details and learning experiences are where the priceless knowledge came from. Asking the right questions is always key.

Where did things start for you? How did you get from starting to advancing? When did you start having children? How did having a family change things? Who were Mentors in your life? What are you passionate about? Are there things you wish you could do over or do again?

Be sure to pay in gratitude for their time and wisdom. Not all Mentors are wealthy in Money. And not all that are Wealthy are necessarily wise. You can learn a lot of things when you listen and stay quiet and can miss out on a lot by speaking too much.

CHAPTER 3

ANYTHING YOU WANT TO LEARN YOU CAN SELF-TEACH YOURSELF. THE LIBRARY HAS ENDLESS KNOWLEDGE.

As with almost everything, Grandpa Thorup was right. You can self-teach yourself literally anything and everything. My grandfather was a self-taught architect. And he had gone from working in the coal mines to working with the Utah Power & Light Company (as named at the time). My Grandfather was proud of education and was in no way anti-college or anti-establishment of learning. He was just all for doing whatever it took to get where you wanted to go. He taught me the value of excuses and that they were worthless. If you could not afford the path, make it. Do whatever you want to do and find a way. There was always a way to get it done. A constant lesson he taught me over and over again as I grew up with his wisdom and voice of reason available to me always.

At the fun age of nine, I was riding my bike to the local city library in Riverton, Utah every Saturday. I was fascinated with computers and was building circuits and Radio Shack kits on everything I could get my hands on.

My grandpa had been taking a liking to the computers and was interested in me. For Christmas that year, he gave my brother, Chan, and I calculator watches. This was a big deal. A watch that was a calculator. It was an expensive gift at the time and my grandmother told me later he had made it possible and was dead set on getting them for us for months. We were the only kids with anything like that at school. I remember having to give it to the math teacher prior to any tests. I also remember being told that we would not have calculators all the time and I would love to point out mine was with me all the time. Amazing how technology has and continues to progress. And now everyone has always at least one calculator with them. Maybe one day the educators can be visionary and promote the possibility of anything.

I also witnessed my grandfather purchasing a TRS80 and shortly after buying it, getting a newer model, and rushing his "now older" model to me to use. He literally set me up on my path to computers, computer telephony and into the internet space to where I have thrived. It was the learning point for me to begin. And I was adapting and growing with the technology as it grew. This was an environmental change that enhanced my mind in huge ways. I will always be grateful for his taking pride in my future.

By the age of 10, I had checked out and read every book there was available on programming in BASIC and understanding computers. It was an interesting time as the government was finally destroying the monopoly known to me at the time as "Mother Bell". Mainly because it was the only telephone company up until this time that had control of everything telephone. This was a huge opening for businesses and free enterprise to begin in telecommunications.

My father created Telephone Service and Supply, a coined reference of respect to my grandfather Edison Ricord's Appliance Service and Supply Company from decades before. At the age of 10, I was assisting and learning how telephones and office telephone systems worked and integrated. It was a poised setting for what was to come. I was punching commercial telephone cables and setting up Office Phone Systems. It was copper wire still and there was not anything digital yet. I was learning the complexities of networks as it developed from commercial phone systems with 2 to 16 lines. From working with single lines coming into a building to watching as T-1's (24 lines) and multiple T-1's to digital fiber and the capacities we have full on internet connected phone systems of today.

I studied computers, telephony, computer telephony and law. The classes I took were in business, accounting, marketing, and business law. High school courses give you some foundation, but it was the self-searching and hitting the library hard that really impacted my learning the most. All the learning I did was proven helpful over and over again. Even the hundreds of hours reading law books and researching new technologies serve me still today.

Grandpa was there for it all. I remember looking into what he did for work and enjoyed how much he loved doing it; architecture and building design. I studied drafting with him. I spent hours perfecting my penmanship as I worked alongside him in his den. Between my mother and grandfather, I studied and took in all I could in structure, penmanship, and design. All of which has served me well throughout life. Every time I hear a compliment on my penmanship, I instantly think of the times I was practicing and practicing by my grandpa's side. There was patience in his work. Something I saw and called the patient process. While I did not gravitate towards drafting, architecture, or engineering, I saw the world differently because of it. There was a finished product that would cover scope and details. My grandpa could see the vision of it before he began. He worked through it, drawing, labeling. All was so precise and perfect. There was a set process to each and every step he took. He was confident from the beginning to the finished design. Watching him work and seeing the finished design unfold was the lesson for me. I took and mirrored the same thought process in virtually everything I set forth to do.

It trained my mind to visualize and know the finished situation. Then I would go about it with the same steps, processes and patience until the vision was complete. I took note of the questions asked and the reasons for the questions. The projects would always be starting out like a puzzle. Understanding the needs and desires of the client took shape and then the puzzle became a vision. Then it was the patient process to complete the design.

My education pushed me through a growth that got me involved with computer telephony, a voice and fax messaging service in 1989 that got me into a career at the age of 15. The learning through self-education and the confidence instilled by my grandfather to learn anything on my own and apply it, always had me figuring out my way.

It was my natural talents and refining through mentors in marketing and sales that allowed me to find a path and run with it. This path led me to Jim Rohn and he, through his time with me at one eventful evening, set me up for all roads leading to wine. Wine being the celebration of what marketing has and continues to allow me to create.

The Internet has already evolved so far that it has eliminated and yet created so many opportunities. The very paths I took and the relationships I have had along the way were oftentimes connected with wine. Several times, in gratitude and respect, I have been given incredible bottles of wine. It has turned into a symbol of celebration and success and many times used to celebrate success.

Taking the same advice from Grandpa in learning and self-teaching from books and Masters of the knowledge before me; wine has been a steady read. Though nothing beats knowledge matched with experience. Fortunately, there is more wine than time and finding that perfect bottle is far more about the road than the completion of the journey.

CHAPTER 4

IF THEY ARE NOT MASTERS OF THE ADVICE YOU ARE LOOKING FOR, FIND THE MASTERS. DO NOT LISTEN TO ANYONE NOT DOING WHAT YOU WANT TO DO.

I am glad to this day that I always thought for myself. I would question anything I did not understand or what did not make logical sense to me. I was not always surrounded by the right individuals to get the answers I sought. And if I felt my questions were inadequately answered or if I could tell my teacher or mentors at the time was without the knowledge; I would seek it elsewhere. Books are amazing. Today, it is still the case and the Internet (along with logic and common sense) makes an amazing resource. Seeking knowledge from a reliable source is easier today than ever and while easy, not everyone does it. I have often been the redeemer of truth to many topics because I would seek out the answers to which I needed. From school teachings to religion and politics. All three of which can be useful if you want a challenge.

We can search for answers in so many ways. From books, to web pages, to incredible videos "showing you step-by-step" how to do just about anything you can imagine. There is a wealth of knowledge and it is growing constantly. It is in-itself a virtual method of value and service to share knowledge with those that seek it and for those yet to seek it. The very nature of our communications to each other is incredible.

I am always amazed at the decisions people will make based on false masters of advice. While the Internet has increased the speed and resources for shared knowledge it has also increased the availability of fools and idiots who speak far more than they themselves listen. There are suddenly experts on anything trending spouting out nonsense. Only to instantly become new experts on something different tomorrow as another topic jumps into the trends.

This is part of human nature that has always baffled me and yet has made my eyes open to the reality of the situations. In life, we all want to achieve and do well. We also have the facts that our environment is 90% of who we are and who we become. We have incredible information and knowledge at our fingertips (and even at our mere asking Alexa a question). Instead of using that resource, we often fall into our environment.

The poor always seem to be poor. The rich always seem to be getting richer. If you want what others have, do what others do. Find a mentor that is doing what you want to do. Find a mentor that has what you want to have. Success leaves clues. Right? If you are seeking advice about a happy relationship or marriage, seek it from someone that has a happy relationship or marriage. If you are looking for advice about starting a business, do not ask someone who has never started a business how to get started. And I am going to really make sure my point gets across here. It is something that I have seen stop so many from even attempting to go after their goals, dreams and even happiness.

For decades now I have been a guide to creating online business. I even built a comprehensive starting, training and full-on support for the online business world. There are students that become frustrated and ready to quit, stopping all of their progress. Their reasons will be because their son, daughter, neighbor, or their friend the auto mechanic told them that everything online is a scam. Instantly they have sought the advice from a mentor that knows absolutely nothing about running an online business.

Seeking the advice from someone that is not doing or is not successful in the subject to which you are seeing information about is not wise. Ever. When you need a lawyer, are you going to go to the baker to have them represent you in court? When your car is not running correctly are you going to call your child's pediatrician to get advice as to what you should do? I certainly would hope not. If you are going to jump out of an airplane for the first time, are you going to jump with someone else that has never done it before either?

Sadly, we often do not go looking for misinformation or advice from those we should not be getting advice from. It usually comes at us freely and often uninvited. It is up to us to filter it out. My suggestion is to be courteous and before giving it any weight or validity ask yourself these three questions.

1. Do they know about the subject you are looking into?
2. Are they successful (currently and not years ago) in the ways you wish to be successful about the subject you are looking into?
3. Are they able to back up their information or advice?

If you cannot answer those with a yes, then you probably want to seek the information elsewhere. There are so many resources and places to go for information. We live in an instant gratification World. We have access to reviews and ratings on almost every business or product out there. And times are changing to make this even more easy to find out.

If a restaurant has bad food, you will know about it by the reviews. If a product is not good, you can find out about reviews in most cases as well. If you are looking into a business, the best research is asking for a customer reference. Can you talk to someone using the product or service?

Making money in the online business world of today is becoming more and more real. There are more people online than ever before. And there will be even more when you finish this chapter. More and more business is growing online and in the way of change and progress with technology. I shudder when I think about all the people that gave up on a way to work for themselves in the growing online business world because their son who is 26 and just graduated with a degree in fine arts is telling them it will never work.

Growing up, I had so many people in my life ask me what I wanted to be when I grew up. I would answer that I wanted to be a millionaire. They would be shocked and other than a few people in my life, the comments looking back were hilarious and stupid. How are you going to do that? Do you have a plan to make that happen? What is your fall back plan if that does not work? And my absolute favorites; you should look into being a doctor or a lawyer then (as if we were playing Life, the board game).

The reasons these questions were hilarious and stupid has nothing to do with the actual questions so much. The reasons all have to do with the people asking them. They were not millionaires (not even close). They were not doctors or lawyers. They were not even striving to be, nor ever were. In fact, no one close to them or around them even were. I did not go up to them to ask them; they brought it up and asked me.

My answer was always that I would figure it out. Everyone knew I was entrepreneurial. I had sold something or many things already to these same individuals. I took their advice as I hoped it was meant, with care and concern. And I gave into the pressure and followed the advice of so many around me "looking out for my best interests". Forget that they themselves weren't looking to be or had ever been a millionaire. I even began a serious path towards being an attorney. Since everyone in my environment, at the time, was so convinced that law or medicine was the sure course for becoming a millionaire.

Thankfully, I read up on everything I could about the laws and being an attorney. I mean, I read every law book available in the city library and county library. It was great knowledge, and it has served me many times.

Mostly though in understanding the process, the structure and how things worked based on case precedents and so forth. I enjoyed the progression into classes such as business law, debate and what I found was that I enjoyed arguing or convincing people. What I did not like was the amount of paperwork and reality of the JOB that working as an attorney truly was. And believe me, I was the better for exiting that path. What it did for me, was in my junior year of high school I got access to the average income by profession. Granted it was two years old at the time, but the average mean income for an attorney was $28k. Not even a close answer to what I was looking for.

Even though my environment was seemingly happy and proud that I had turned to law in seeking my millionaire desire, it was not the answer. Stats and numbers have always been my friend. Numbers do not lie, but the intention of others sure do. Fortunately, the time invested in reading, researching, learning the legal processes; all of it was helpful. Legal situations in business are a matter of when and not if. Especially when you gain ground and start building.

For me, I enjoyed the marketing and sales processes far more than doing paperwork and working with the legal system. For me, I needed to find mentors in business, particularly those that could market and make sales happen. This led me to Richard Davidson and then an entire series of mentors. Once my course was set and I focused on becoming the best version of me, mentors appeared. Literally. I would seek them and as I grew my businesses, I would find them. And now I get to pass the information and knowledge forward.

And I will keep seeking mentors that have what I want and can show me how to change and grow even more. Learning is vast and our lives are so short. Pushing to gain the most out of life and to create and leave a legacy behind. This has become the importance I truly seek now. How many people, families, communities can I help become better. As I hit walls, I merely seek the mentor to get me through, under or around those walls. Solutions are always out there. Always.

CHAPTER 5

IT IS DIFFICULT TO BE A KING IN YOUR OWN BACKYARD.

Well, this is going to be a fun chapter. It also is going to be a huge kick in the ass of success for many. I have studied and studied people. For hours and hours in single days. Watching them from a marketing and sales perspective. I have been mentored by incredible speakers, motivational trainers, and highly successful people in many areas of life. I have found that doing something great in the city, town, or community you grew up in is difficult.

It all has to do with perception. I had a mentor who was very educated. He was on the board of the Computer Telephony Company I was the sole marketer for. He spoke five languages fluently and was sought after by many international firms. Of all the times we broke bread, discussed things, and travelled together; one thing he said has helped me tremendously. It has been a foundational point of understanding in almost everything I do in the way of marketing. It is the foundation to which I always begin. And it belongs here for the sheer fact that it sums up this entire chapter in three words. Perception is reality.

The perception of those you are looking to market to and then sell to matters the most. Not what your perception is. What we ourselves perceive is where our reality lies. Right or wrong. Same goes for the customer or potential customer. While perception is reality; it is also something you must never forget. It is the main concern with anything to be marketed. And this is where we start with you and being a king in your own backyard.

See, we grow up, develop who we are to become; typically, within the same circles of influence for most of our lives. Our family, our friends, neighbors, and community. These very people that we grew up with and in front of us are "perception biased". They will have a perception of you that is bound by your childhood. They will be so biased that they will not see the growth and capacities you have as you become a better you. They will only see that kid that hit a baseball thru their window. That girl who wore pigtails in elementary school. They will see you for the worst parts of you out of bias. Peers will not want you to do better than them and will naturally root against you. Family can be even more harsh.

The perceptions of the wealthy in income and life balance are far different. There is an amazing growth and understanding as you allow yourself to achieve. Unfortunately, this is where things are not equal for all. Those with environments that are not of wealth and abundance in all things will have a whole different perception and support (or lack of) and while it is sad, it is perception. And therefore, it is a reality. You can overcome this, however.

See, it is human nature for the lesser abundant and wealthy minded individuals to give a total stranger more credibility than someone they watched grow up. A perfect stranger will be given far more benefit of the doubt and an ear to speak too, especially with a new idea. Knowing this allows you to adjust and to offer a way to win. It is bringing in a third party to endorse the new idea or business. And while you will need this in your own Environment; you will be the same support and third party to endorse for others in the same way.

You will find it easier to build with like-minded strangers that you meet for the first time, rather than those from your established environment. This is also why I will have a trusted partner explain any new idea or business to someone I know rather than present it myself. For it is only when someone else edifies you and your part in a new idea or business; that someone can allow their perception to be changed. And therefore, their reality to be changed. Because it is a new person, they will genuinely give them more respect than you. It is an odd but true perception. And since "perception is reality" after all, who presents does matter.

This entire reasoning behind "perception is reality" and the fact that you cannot be a king in your own backyard is also an explanation why marketing is not an overnight success. It takes time, something I call the patient process. When building a business or sharing a new idea to your existing environment; knowing what you are up against is key. It is not impossible, but it takes more time than dealing with complete strangers. I consider it a thermometer of success. For when those from your environment become open and supportive; know you have done your marketing well. Also do not count on it, but absolutely celebrate it.

It was years before people from my environment to which I grew up were coming to me for new ideas or business directions. In fact, it may have been decades before it became anything steady. This is why the vast reach of the Internet keeps giving and giving. Anything I tend to pursue should have a national if not global reach. Based upon numbers and stats alone, the bigger your reach the bigger your odds of success. And since the Internet is only growing in users, global reach and constantly growing, it only makes sense to be a part of it. It is just too large not to be.

Even if you are a small boutique store in a small town, the internet gives you access to the globe. Use it.

CHAPTER 6

IF IT WERE EASY, EVERYONE WOULD BE DOING IT.

Many wish things to be easier, where they should wish that they themselves would become better. Solutions are where the value lies in life. Almost every product or service out there is a solution to a problem or need. If you have a problem where you are not where you want to be in life, then you need a solution. That solution may not be the easiest of things. Why? Because if it were easy, then everyone would be doing it. I look at this from any product or service. And there are two incredible sides of understanding to this. The initial side is the one we all see; how it impacts us. The other is how it impacts others and where the large opportunity of any issue lies. Bear with me here. This is deep, but so valid. And while you may need to read this many times, it is the core understanding that allows you to see why you cannot ever quit. It always gets better as you get better.

I have always been a believer of figuring out a system. Call it a routine even. With anything, the more you do it the better you become. Muscle memory, thought, attitude and expectations all become a known fact through repetition. What you do becomes what you receive. Anything becomes easier and easier with practice. Our brains are incredible. They figure things out and get faster and faster at doing the same things as before.

"Don't wish it was easier, wish you were better." Jim Rohn

When you start out with anything, it starts awkwardly and gets better and better. Soon you are conquering things in ways that look easy to an outsider looking in; but it is merely the perfecting of the system, the process, the routine. When you take something hard, make it look easy and then share the rewards of it all, everyone will want to be doing it. If you are doing the "hard" you can enjoy the financial gains of when "everyone is doing it".

Let us look at a solution that was not easy initially. The laptop computer. It started out as a way to create a portable way to take a computer on the road. Not easy. Required batteries and screens and the main computer. All sorts of issues needed to be solved. Packaging, better and smaller everything. Keyboards, screens, batteries, fans, CPUs, motherboards. Everything needed to become more and more compact. The problems being solved were countless. The costs were prohibited to many if not most initially. As the routine of portable computers became more and more common; more and more got involved. The more that got involved, the more solutions that came to make it easier and easier. Systems were put in place to create smaller, faster portable computer solutions. Then they are improved on and through competition and of course a never-ending demand; they only become better and better.

Years later we have portable computing far faster, smaller, and far better. Adoption to the masses became easier and easier and therefore everyone is doing it. Laptops, Smartphones, Tablets, Wearables. If it becomes easy, everyone will be doing it. Not only is this a testament to the processes, but where incredible opportunity is created and available.

I will further explain the details. Computers going portable started out far from easy. It started out very difficult. I met some of the innovators of portable computing. They literally ran a computer from the back of a van. Not small, not easy at all. But they had a power source in the running van powering the batteries for the computer that was portable only because it fit in the back of the van; to handle their client's needs. They travelled to remote locations where power was not available. This was far from easy. And it was almost ridiculous. It was so much work, but they had to figure it out. They were a solution to a big need. This led to more and more seeing the value and then the solutions came to make it easier and easier. Then as more and more realized the need for portable computers, solutions were created. These solutions created jobs, economies, and countless opportunities.

The idea of a portable computer was not a huge need at first. It was not a realized need by the masses initially. These innovators had it hard. Star Trek with its communicators was science fiction at the time. And as time went by and more and more solutions were solved by portable computers, the easier things became. The easier things became, the more people were jumping in. Why, because someone did the hard. Be grateful for hard, because where things are hard, there are opportunities.

Economically, some of us remember our first laptops costing $9000 or more. Not exactly an easy purchase for many. And the other side of if was easy, everyone would be doing it. The more we need something, the more solutions become available. The more that get involved with these solutions the more competition in creating these solutions are created. And then supply and demand can meet, "hard" in cost becomes "easy" in cost as more enter the solution space.

Today as you read this, you probably have 10 to 20 portable computers or more that you use in your everyday life. Maybe more. It is so easy that literally everyone is using them. Everyone you would say is doing it.

Fast forward to today. The Internet and way of life both personal and business is becoming a new "easy". Some of us have been working towards this digital solution for all things marketing for some time. It hasn't been easy. It is becoming easy. And yes, soon everyone will be doing it.

Proper business development and marketing systems take something that is hard and time consuming and allow it to become easier and faster. Basically, the system takes a hard idea, hard process and makes it easy so that everyone can do it. I have been around processes that took 12 years for a person to achieve a certain level of success. It was hard work by anyone's measure. As the hard was done and processes refined it became easier. As the desire for the outcome increased, proper marketing systems were added and the entire process that once took12 years took two years. Now that it was easier at two years, others began doing it in 18 months and even within one year.

The opportunity for those that did the hard work, even though it took 12 years, allowed them to refine it and make it easier. This is how innovation makes things better by making it go from hard to easy.

This is how leadership works too. Leading is not easy. Think about it. First you need people to lead. And it starts with you. If you cannot lead yourself on a path, then how are you going to lead another person? If you cannot lead a person, how are you going to lead people? We start out by creating a routine, a system of doing the task at hand. Then we lead ourselves and then others. The more we do it, the more we improve and the easier it becomes. The easier it becomes the more that can "do it". True and good leaders gain in the rewards their team creates. The opportunity of making "hard" turn into "everyone can do it," can be truly incredible.

Where we start, is where we will determine where we end. From hard to easy. From A to B. It must start somewhere. Then you progress and allow your brain to learn, your muscles and habits to form and allow it to become easy. Start with Integrity, Honesty and in doing things correctly. Starting out is hard. Starting out right or wrong is still hard. Right is right and will always be right. Wrong is always Wrong and should never be done. If it's worth doing, it's worth doing right. Truth is easy, we all can do truth.

Many of the things I have shared within these pages were hard and then became easy. May they find their way of ease to you. I cannot explain the joy and happiness received from it all. It continues and I genuinely want to share it with everyone I can.

Life is a gift and what we do with that gift is truly everything. I fully know that we will be judged and honored in the next phases of life based upon what we do with the gifts and life we have here and now. And this is exactly how I believe and conduct myself with each and every project, program or Opportunity I take part in.

The ability to take something hard and make it easy is something that itself started out hard (almost feeling impossible even) and became easier the more I worked at it. To where the Systemization and Teaching Principles became instant.

There are certain things that cannot be automated. High Touch items such as building the actual client relationship. But all the things that support the building of the relationship can be automated. Technology can connect the high touch actions with the reminders, the follow ups and the engagements. The experience can be fully developed and made easy.

I have been able to steer many into success by creating a process and utilizing systems to automate everything that can be automated. Then the High Touch aspects remain but are easier to become "easy". Just a matter of following the system. Allowing the processes, and technology pieces within the system to do their part.

Removing the issues that take up time and are not part of the High Touch needs of the Process; allows the High Touch to become easier and easier. Training and development on automation tools becomes easier too. And then it always comes down to the actual High Touch aspects of marketing, client acquisition and client retention.

Just wait, soon you will have the marketing understanding. When Marketing is done properly, sales becomes "order taking." Proper marketing by itself is an automated System taking what is arguably the "hardest" aspect of any business, product or service and turning it into perfection and "ease".

Then not only does it become easy from previously being hard; but something everyone can be doing. Which is both the initial issue and the final goal. Making the hard easy and making it easy for those that follow the path of ease created by those that designed the system for success.

Just like with the laptop or portable computer. You could take a tower pc, a monitor, a keyboard and make it work in the back of a van. Have it run off the battery of the van. Or you could now purchase a portable computer for your needs. One with a built-in battery, keyboard, monitor, CPU, fan, and hard drive to function fully as the computing device you need. The portable computer is the developed system that made it easy.

CHAPTER 7

EMOTIONS ARE A LUXURY WE CANNOT AFFORD.

This chapter may need an entire bottle of Cabernet Sauvignon (We will call it Cab for short). Mainly because Cab is so enjoyable to drink, you will be drinking it often; just as keeping your emotions in check will be something you will do often. This is important because the knowledge I am about to drive home in this chapter is something you will want to remember every time you are drinking a Cab. This is an important life lesson that has truly helped me from myself over and over again.

My largest mistakes had emotion spilled all over them. And the biggest rebounds and recoveries had emotions removed from them almost entirely. Emotions are some of the most challenging roadblocks we all face every day. Ironically, they are also what makes us human and are the cause for everything we do. We do not get out of bed without emotions. Without emotions we would do nothing.

Emotions are where wasted time, money and opportunity are consumed into an endless black hole of regrets. This was a hard lesson. Mainly because when I fully understood it, I had already lived through an expensive course of life, all due to emotions. I am a passionate person and that has its rewards for sure. It also comes with a side of emotional expenses that would amaze you.

I had a Chief Technical Officer that was an incredible mentor in many aspects, the most memorable were in the truths of life. And this is absolutely one of the most amazing lessons I could pass along to anyone. It has been an incredible change in my own understanding that only bettered me. I can tell you that the benefits are not just monetary, but in all aspects of life. Especially where it matters the most, in the family and relationships of those we hold dear.

See, any and all regret is tied to an emotion. They are very expensive. And if you are not understanding it, go sit in any courtroom and listen to the lives disrupted, lost, or ruined because of emotion. We make decisions based on emotion and when logic prevails it is not always the same wishful outcome.

When I find that I am emotionally charged up on a decision, I slow it down. Whether it is regarding our children, or a business matter, I slow it down. Time is the adjustment. Nothing good comes from charged emotional reactions. All things good are good now and tomorrow. Nothing must happen in a split second other than life and death decisions. And with that exception, I will continue.

In life and dealing with our loved ones, or co-workers, bosses, or colleagues; emotions need to remain in check. This is where wealth is not always measured in money. Wealth in patience and control is without measure. It is priceless. Truly. Less is more and he (or she) who loses their temper last wins. Believe me, when a man or woman in business understands this life's truth, anything is possible. I have also found that the energy that is created from the knowledge I am about to explain has rewards in all areas of your life.

Almost any decision can be made tomorrow. I am not talking about procrastination. We all know when it is time to take action. TAKE IT. But when things get emotional, mind you… slow it down. When we jump to conclusions, assume things out of rage and emotion, things get messy 99% of the time. This mess costs us in time, respect and as a result, income, and opportunity.

Because we are human, we have emotions. Because of emotions we do everything. The control of emotions lies the power and where mindset creates advantages for gains. Just like we all have 24 hours in each and every day, we all share the same access to emotions and what we do with them.

Avoid the tornado. This alone has saved me in countless hours of regret. Just like mother nature, emotions can create a tornado. Step away, remove yourself. Take cover and wait for the storm to consume itself and pass. When someone else is wrapped up in an emotional tornado they are twisted up and damaging everything around them. Step away, slow down and do not jump in. Protect yourself and wait. When the storm calms down, it will clear up and decisions will be easier. Do not buy into the rage of the tornado.

You will see drama and lies are best used against us in a storm. The deceit of emotionally charged experiences are never good. Plus, when you learn the power of being in control and waiting for the storm to pass, you will see less of them. We truly teach others how to treat us by our reactions to their actions.

When a child is throwing a temper tantrum, slow things down. Wait it out. Then proceed. Same goes with teenagers, adults, and almost all situations. Same things goes with how we react in our homes, careers, business, pleasure and really everything.

It can be a loved one, or a complete stranger. Things happen. It is how we react that allows for the results. Problems, frustrations, issues of all kinds can arise. We react and then the outcome follows. Reacting from a relaxed patient perspective is always better than a charged up emotional response. We can take time to weigh out the desired outcomes. And we can avoid looking like an idiot to match the person that was in the emotional tornado.

Any decision in life based upon the logic of the outcome is better than one made with emotion. Sound decisions in life only become better with emotion after they are sound. This is something I have seen become true time and time again since I fully understood and utilized this truth.

Make a List. Pros and Cons of the decision. Logically think it out. Look at the impact on your life and finances before jumping in. Sound decisions are almost always the ones without emotional fluff added in.

Let us say you are going to buy a new car. Your current car is about paid off and running just fine. Sure, it has wear and tear and maybe you think you could attract a better partner in life if you had a more fun, faster, sexier car. You also (and because it only makes sense if you are reading this book) are looking to be stronger financially for the future as well. So hopefully we can break for an emotional and logical self-check before deciding on a new car. Let us write out the pr's and cons. Here is exactly how I would do this based upon my habits and view on things. Mind you, I did not always understand this. Okay, let us do this.

Pros:

- It is a brand-new car.
- I will look incredible in a new car.
- People will see me as richer than when I was in my old car.
- I will have a warranty on the new car.

Cons

- My old car if paid off / only has x payments left.
- The new car will cost me x for x months.
- My budget will be x less each month to cover the car payment.
- My Insurance will go up from x to y with this new car.

The difference in monthly expenses will go from x to y by changing my old car to the new car.

Now based upon these things it should be making sense logically, not emotionally. If it is just emotions and the desire to have a new car, let us be realistic. If you want the ability to invest and grow, you will affect your monthly cash flow with this decision. Also, the car you drive is a social status symbol. However, so are your debts. And the more you need to spend to maintain your possessions the less you must invest into growing your financial position.

The same goes for any purchase that is going to be put on credit. Credit cards are used by most people as a way to gain instant gratification. You do not have the money to buy it today, but you want it today. So, you use your credit to buy it now and then pay for it with interest over time. The life of installment payments. This is where the financial demise of almost anyone begins. You create a situation where your available funds each month dwindle away to pay for things you received long ago. Soon you no longer can buy anything on money you have today, and you are buying things on the future incomes' months or years later. Not exactly a recipe for financial success. It is a sure way to dig a hole that many never get out of.

This is where patience and removal of emotions become activities of wealth creation. Emotions in this aspect of life are more expensive than people want to believe. The extra $10, $50, $100, $200 a month you start building up in interest payments go against you and your quality of life.

If you do not absolutely need it, don't buy it on credit. If you cannot afford it today, you logically cannot afford it tomorrow either. If you are financially strapped today, then why would you want to be further strapped tomorrow?

Credit cards are credit lines. They are best used to create instances of cash flow. Using the bank's money to create cash flow, or in other words business income. I have been working with employee minded people for decades. And I'll break down the use of a credit card for those looking to be a great employee and working towards the long-term plan of being an employee for a great employer.

Being an employee, you more or less have a set Income. There are needs to your employment that need to be met for your employment and are expected. These are needs. Dress code will require you dress a certain way. You will need clothing to adhere to this standard. You will need transportation to and from your work (unless you are working from home). Fuel and maintenance costs are part of self-transportation, etc. Meals while you are at work, etc.

These are all costs to you that come from your set income. Should you not have these when you begin your work and should you not have the funds to get them out of cash, then using a line a credit (or a credit card) makes sense. It is the available resources to invest in what you need to secure the set income you will receive. This is cash flow. Now buying a new video game system is probably not anywhere in the needs category for your Set Income and therefore is not necessary.

The key is to spend what you need (without emotion). Your home or housing, food, clothing, transportation. The remainder you are the steward. Invest, save, do the things you need to do to get what you want to get. Anything you do for entertainment, is where emotions come in. The more you save and invest, the more you can have in your retirement years. That is the basic laid out plan of understanding. As you make decisions that use up more money for the needs, the less you must invest or save, and so on.

Having a set income has its pros. You are knowledgeable about what you must work with week to week, month to month. You can make your decisions based on that. And barring being fired, let go, furloughed, or otherwise upset in your set income, you know what is to work with. The cons are the same. You are limited.

Having time and money. If you have time outside of the time you trade in for the set income, you have a pathway to create more Income. If you have credit you have a line of credit to use to build additional incomes. That is if you are not emotionally tying up those for instant gratification and paying for things with interest and digging holes into financial despair. That new couch looks amazing, but the loss of credit to build cash flow could have bought you a new couch every month in six months from now if used properly.

For those that are self-employed entrepreneurs, or business owners, the use of credit cards or lines of credit need to cover things in different ways. We need to look the part; we need to cover the life needs and we need to create the business that creates the cash flow. The risk is different, but so are the available gains.

Now if you are with a set income and you have funds to invest or a credit card to use as a line of credit to create cash flow, this is where the rich can become richer. It is also where the "employee" can cross over to wealth creation in the business and creation directions.

Time is the equalizer for everyone. 24 hours a day, no one gets more or less. Emotions can cost us in time. If you create or have friends that create drama in your life, you are letting emotional costs take your time. Expensive. So often you will see a financially strapped, or broke person spending their time in non-cash-flow creating ways. Having drama, or social media, television, or binges in sports, movies, or whatever is only costing your future. It is all emotional filler. And it is all costly. Anyone not seeing that is already in a "broke" mentality. Their future is most likely not financially secure.

Now take your available time, whether full time or part time and apply it to creating cash flow. This is where you can get your money and time working for you. Today more than ever there are some incredible ways to create wealth. In fact, creating multiple streams of income is "easy" today. The "hard" has already been done. You just need to follow the right mentors, use the right systems, and give it your best.

Take the time savings from utilizing systems and automation tools to apply to High Touch solutions for your business. Prioritize your available time to focus on money making activities. These are where you are creating cash flow. Cash flow that comes in weekly or monthly is the same net effect of having thousands, hundreds of thousands, millions, tens of millions or more in the bank paying interest to you. It is all in the leverage of wealth creation. It is so much more rewarding than any television program you could ever watch.

Additionally, having the patience to build up a solid and growing cash flow allows for far more than new cars. And when you are solid financially and have it together, the problems and emotions of life will not leave you. You will be even more attractive than you were, and your energy will change to attract other lessons in life. This is where we could share some life's stories and would each need a bottle of something fun like a Tanya Pinot Grigio. Add in a plate of grapes, blueberries, strawberries and some Swiss, Havarti and some soft cheeses and we can discuss it all for hours on a bright afternoon.

Life and life's Issues are far more entertaining and enjoyable with financial strength. The irony of it all, is when you learn to remove emotions to make the cash flow happen; emotions later are far more enjoyable to experience. They come with a silver lining of freedom. Achieve this, and you will completely understand.

Financial strength removes the emotions of being broke and you can really make better decisions in all areas of life without the emotions of being broke or "strapped" financially. The summary to this chapter could be summed up as all decisions in life when you are not financially sound are emotions. Emotions will cost you dearly. Remove the financial straps and remove the need for emotions; allowing you a sounder mind to make decisions with.

SECTION II

CHANGING MINDSET AND PRIORITIES

CHAPTER 8

WHY SHOULD IT BE LONELY AT THE TOP?

One of the most gut-wrenching statements I have heard many times in my life from leaders and respected people touted as experts is that "it's lonely at the top." Though that statement may be evident and truthful, it should not be. It has always twisted up my stomach. Always.

It goes against my core beliefs and understandings of life and life's purpose. From Christ to Allah there is never meant for just a few to rise up. We are meant to work and progress together. Strength in numbers. We are meant to be leaders.

We are not here to climb up on the backs of others. We are here to rise, grow and help each other to ascend to greatness. We adapt, we learn, we follow in truth and right. As we progress in growth as a society, we should be creating a way to increase the quality of life for all.

If I achieve incredible success and only help my family and myself, that is one thing. However, to help thousands and thousands to achieve success;

well, that must be far greater of an achievement. If it is hard, then by sheer repetition hard becomes easy. Proper teaching and leadership can help any concept be easier for many.

Likewise, for any adaptable and available path of success. When it comes to any aspect of business, there must be a better way to help more to achieve more. For this is the true innovation of what is available. Let us break it down.

The corporate structure of old. It is a sham of issues. Subject to all sorts of failures to those doing the work to make things happen. I am not a fortune teller or psychic; however, I can see the change that is already happening. Especially when I have been a part of it. And it is just like anything that is filled with truth. It will rise to the top. It will conquer. It will become the NEW.

Knowledge and the understanding and use of the knowledge is where it can all happen. The new or what sounds impossible becomes the way of it all. Hard becomes easy. And when it is easy, we all can do it.

So, take the corporate structure that is constructed on a caste system. Owners, management, managers, and employees. This is becoming a joke, and not exactly a beacon of true freedom. And the new way is able to wipe it away with innovations, technologies and shared passions with all that participate including the customer.

More than ever the connection from the product to the customer is becoming less and less in moving pieces. Marketing is becoming everything, and the support and "love" is cementing the relationships. Experience of the client is being broadcast in real time through emotions and experiences. These transparencies have changed the model of business. It has also allowed for the new way of things to progress. A new way to better things for anyone really.

No longer does it need to be a place where the employer makes money on the backs of the least paid employee being the face of the company. The people will always be the most incredible asset of any business. The heart and soul of any business is the love and care of those running the business.

With that, the new is where there is proportional gain to all involved and the ones that cement the relationship with the clients gain. As we break this down, we create a place where the energies and passions of all can create more of a win overall.

Take what used to be seen as an employer to employee relationship and create partnerships. Where the gain from success is shared overall. And make it proportionate to the results created by the "partner" in the partnership. The owner/entrepreneur creates the opportunity and shares the successes with those that make it happen. Limits are endless and results equate to rewards for all.

Can you imagine a shopping and customer experience where the employees gain from the happiness and client experience? Where frustrating a customer instantly influences the earnings and rewards of the entire store? What will happen when the success of each store becomes the success of every partner working within the store? Some may issue stocks or allow stock incentives. More and more I see the evolution of partner-based outcomes in the companies that will lead in their sectors in years to come.

As people seek out places to trade their time for earnings, they will seek the places that create happiness. Happiness in the daily experience and payments for their participation in the partnership with them and the company.

Things clicked into place for my enterprises as I created opportunities that rewarded the efforts of the partners that joined with me. The more I press on building up my partners in education, understanding and self-improvement the better we all do. The overall rewards only grow. The top truly becomes filled with more and more, not fewer.

Being lonely at the top is not the right way of things. It is merely the visibility of the goal to take as many as you can with you. The happiness felt when getting to the top is nothing as compared when you truly help others to come with you. And as the hard becomes easy, soon everyone will be doing it.

CHAPTER 9

COLLECTED REALITIES TO THE FUNDAMENTALS OF WEALTH CREATION

This is a nice—and possibly extra-long—title for a chapter, I admit. I also admit that it took me several mistakes and somewhat wasted time to get to these realities. I trust that my time in figuring out these realities will aid you in saving time figuring these things out on your own, or that it will at least open your mind to where you will understand and see that you already understood this, and that it just needed to be pointed out.

We have all heard that you need your money working for you and investing with interest is powerful. That is all great for those that have made it happen, but this is not the case for most people. There are huge numbers of populations within the world's richest countries who are not gaining from this, let alone in the third world countries.

The reality that people need is in an understanding of how to fix things going forward and doing this from the position of not having any money to invest. We need to break it down by time and how to use it to change the actions of today for actions of tomorrow. That will allow for wealth creation.

If you are trading your time for money, you are never going to get ahead. Time is valuable and is the one equality we all start with. Each day we are blessed with comes with the same 24 hours for each of us. What you do with your 24 hours and what I do with my 24 hours are probably different and therefore will give us different results. We can gain and get results based upon what we invest in timewise.

Getting ahead is changing your time and income negotiations, from dollars for hours to dollars for actions. The more you are utilizing your time and resources to create income and wealth on actions versus time, the better. The reality? You need to get away from time for money and get money for actions. Then, use your time efficiently and smartly to make more actions in the time available.

If we work a job for $20 an hour and work eight hours a day, we are looking at $160 a day. Five days a week is $800 per week. Now, adding an hour commute each way costs two more hours. Add an hour lunch, and now we have 11 hours spent. With eight hours sleeping we only have five hours remaining. One to get ready each morning and four for your needs.

Remove the two hours of commuting. Say you utilize the incredible technologies we have and work from your home. No commuting. Instantly, four hours for your needs now becomes six. We won't discuss the savings from transportation and social additions of clothing and more. Just the time. Those six hours can be utilized to create income that is not based on your time as it overcomes the income generated by the eight hours of pay for time traded; you can begin the wealth creation and accumulation that is based on actions and not time.

Now, take those four or six hours and work smart to build something that can grow with technology. Replace your income created from time to leveraging systems. If you are unable to work from home, then so be it. We will work with the hours you have available. When the hard becomes easy, you can create more from leverage than from your set time, allowing you to be able to get ahead.

If you are not creating income without trading time for it, you are in a broken state of wealth. You are not working in a smart direction to build income. You are only gaining income for time traded, and you have a set income based on the amount of time you can trade for income. You will never have more than 24 hours in a day—and if you ever find a way to do that, please get in contact with me first. I'll openly admit to being wrong and will jump on in!

Take those four hours, those six—whatever you have—and apply them to a better and new way to create income. These hours are now the most important asset you have. What you do with them will determine the life and rewards you have. Do you watch television or social media, trading them for zero gains in income? Or do you take that time and invest it in yourself? Work with something you can build and get paid based upon actions, making things happen and supporting the growth that can happen by building in an environment of entrepreneurism paid on results.

As you do this, the new direction will become the only direction, and the realities of it will allow you to do something that can not only change your wealth, but how you see wealth. Then, expand it to your children and loved ones and see how it changes their wealth. This is where the value of our time is met with the value we give it.

Now, if you take those same four-to-six hours of time and watch television, social media or spend them in non-money-making-activities, you will be spending time without wealth reward. This is something to balance. We have health and wealth, and within it we have the resources of time. Exercise, nutrition, and quality of life all balance out., but the quality of life without wealth is never what we deserve. We truly deserve to have it all.

We just need to utilize our resources in a manner that allows wealth to happen, and there are solutions that allow this to happen. With the way the world is changing, it is becoming easier for more to participate.

Learning the processes and systems, and understanding what it takes to create Cash Flow, is one thing. As you apply it to multiple streams of income, it can open up security and assurances for your future.

CHAPTER 10

UNMEASURED TIME IS LOST TIME

Thankfully, I was raised by both my mother and grandfather who were precise with most everything. Schedules and structure to even the smallest of daily tasks. The amount of activity and accomplishments that they both achieved daily were to me, always amazing. They did not let the moss grow under their feet and they made great use of the time given them. I appreciate this part of the upbringing and yet colliding views with marketing and off-kilter approaches challenged my learning on this matter. I'll bring this to a full understanding when we get into chapter 25. And it will probably be something that will definitely be a cause for a restless night or two as you reflect on how it has affected your life and buying decisions. Sometimes being a marketer is also being a magician. Magicians make it look like magic. Really it is a well versed and applied understanding of what the prospect is looking at, looking for and delivering it in a manner that the prospects is jumping at becoming a client. They go from looking into it to wanting it, needing it… and needing it now.

The success of any product, service, or business, is directly tied to the marketing success behind them. Marketing is being a magician and solving the question from the client: "what is in it for me?" To pull off the magic is not just wonderment; it is making the hard easy and making the results organized and scalable. It is figuring out many things through trial and error. It is creating a process, a system, and a way to have it all come together and for the client to see it themselves. This is the magic of it. And face it, we all enjoy magic.

I have found that true marketing minds understand many aspects of life and living beyond other typical or common mindsets. The understanding of your client, potential client and how to be the solution for the needs they have is far more than what is on the surface.

We all have 24 hours of time to use every blessed and brilliant day. When you look at those that have what you want to have, you may find a path of how they got there. You can do this by comparing what you do with those that have what you want do with the same 24 hours of every day.

Marketing is one of the largest professions. It encompasses so many things. It is emotional, it is logical, it is a solution-based direction at almost every turn. There are more solutions to issues from marketing than most any profession. Each and every profession needs marketing. Nothing sells itself. And repeatedly:

"Marketing done properly makes sales become order taking." - Rory Ricord

There is a direct correlation to success and time management. Every business, every product and service are better marketed with a strict focus on the time management side of it all. And nothing happens as fast as you would like. Patience and marketing success are connected.

A lot of things done in marketing are done for a long period of time and in a steady (non-ending) manner. This is something that takes absolute time. It needs to be accounted for, measured, and prioritized. As does anything of importance. Marketing is freedom. And it is something that like air is needed all the time for us to live and maintain. Think about it. Without marketing, nothing progresses or is shared. We need to consume things to live. Always. By this, freedom is created and maintained. It is incredible.

To get the most out of anything, you need to plan for it. This is also the main area where my students have made the mistakes to get into their own way. Success is begging for us. It is the natural way of things. Solutions want to find us. The universe is about growth and betterment. We just need to lay out the path to help it run into us.

If you do not structure your time, you will take longer to make anything happen. Success is planned and not accidental. Even in today's technology a written day planner is sometimes a key to making your success happen. The written word is powerful and declaring it into a schedule is something worth doing.

If it is in the calendar it exists. If it is not in the calendar it might not happen. Time management allows for you to become busy. Busy people get things done. The proper use and visualization of your time and time spent allows you to be structured. This structure allows for you to weigh out priorities and to allow you to pack in your day. It allows you to measure your time.

Measured time is where the same 24 hours is better utilized by those who measure and appreciate it. Unmeasured time will slip by and be forever lost. Plan the day and own it. Use the time you were blessed with today to make tomorrow better.

CHAPTER 11

RESET, REFOCUS, RECOMMIT

RRR, which is short for Reset, Refocus, Recommit, is what I discovered and use in my life to bounce up from getting knocked down or distracted. It is all about creating the habits that allow you to create success. It is something that I have watched people benefit from. It's all about having the correct habits.

I thoroughly enjoy this part of my instruction with my students. It is something best taught in a live setting and through the conveyance of energy and tones throughout a physical exercise of these very tools. It is effective in helping to grow and become better in all aspects of life. When you have a calm temperament and the mental tools to make things happen, true happiness and the freedom of this happiness can be realized. RRR.

See, we all have the same 24 hours in each day. Those who take measure and truly value their time are better set up for success to meet them along the journey. Habits are the tools necessary to navigate each and every minute of time. Efficiency is honing in on the time and maximizing the effort and results.

Two people can set forth an hour to do a task. The manners of efficiencies and discipline set forth will determine the end results and outcomes of the work at hand. How we go about the very task in the time allotted is crucial. It will become a habit when discipline is involved.

Then, staying on task and the manner of how we do the functions, tasks, and steps of the task kick in. And with all things come the distractions and habits of distractions. This includes the rabbit holes of social media, the diversion of a relationship, and emotions.

As these things get into our path, we need to get back to the task at hand and we need to do this in a manner that is going to allow us to stay on task, stay on focus, stay committed. This is where the RRR comes in. It may need to be done several times in the course of a day, an hour and sometimes minutes. This is a mental exercise that starts out hard for everyone. The more you do it, the easier and faster it becomes.

Reset

This is where this mental exercise begins. To do this you need to put yourself into a calm and clear space. This will take time at first. Soon, it will become a faster and easier process. This will help in many ways and aspects of your life. Setting you up for increased productivity, success, happiness, and freedom.

Put yourself into a state of calm. I mentally go to a white snowy field. Or to a beach. If you have never been in snow, the beach will work. It is helpful if you have been there before so you can utilize your memories to visualize it best. For the white snow, I imagine myself in a white field of snow. As I do this, anything that gets my mind distracted I turn into a tree, a rabbit, a twig, and then I cover it with the snow. I do this until I am in a state of complete calm with nothing but a perfect landscape of snow.

If I mentally go to the beach, I go to soft sands where nothing is there but the sand. The interruptions become holes or seashells in the sand, only to be covered up and smoothed over by the sand as the waves wash over them. I get to where the sand is calming and all I see is sand.

This is the Reset. It is where you slow things down and remove the noise and interruptions and then get back to your focus and commitment. It truly does not matter how many times you get rattled off your course; what matters is that you always find one more way to get back on course and get to it.

Refocus

Once you are in a clear state of mind you want to ask the “why” and “focus” of the work that you set forth to do. The reasons--the whys--are what you are truly focusing on. Something has removed you from your clear path and focus. Now we have cleared our mind and we are Refocusing back into place.

Recommit

Once we have Refocused, we Recommit to doing what we set forth to do. We Recommit to getting it done. Then, we act.

It is necessary to repeat these three steps until the task is complete. These are tools and habits that allow you to get things done. Regardless of what is thrown our way, we get back to the task. We Reset, Refocus and Recommit to it. From small tasks to large tasks and every size of task in-between.

These are the very tools that have allowed the impossible to become possible. The very tools that have allowed prosperity and success during depression, divorce, death of loved ones and so many other diversions. It is not what happens to us, but how we choose to deal with it that matters.

CHAPTER 12

RRR IN EVERYDAY LIFE - RRR247

From tasks with work, your business, and in your daily life, the RRR is a tool that will help you get the most out of each and every morsel of time you have daily. Along with planning and measuring your time, RRR will allow you to gain much more out of life.

There are countless obstacles and challenges I have faced in my journey for wealth, happiness, and freedom. They still come up all the time. The more I give and help others, the more obstacles and challenges that come up. It is part of the journey of life. It is also a great reminder that mind over matter and the ability to use the tools of RRR can get you past it all.

I can tell you it is one of the best things, that was hard at first but becomes easy. It is a habit, a way of handling the crap that life throws at us. It is also something that money cannot buy. It is created from patience and removing emotions to clear a path to get back to what you want. It is a way to take control of everything you can control and move ahead.

It really is something to appreciate. And the little wins of completing the tasks in spite of the obstacles makes the celebration that much better. When we complete the day and have our glass of wine, the taste of a successful day is better and better with each RRR experienced along the way.

These tasks being completed are all part of a focus and commitment to bettering yourself, your deserved rewards, and your freedom. Celebrating even the tiniest of wins is important to realize the next new day and press forward to it.

We are always in competition with ourselves to become the best us we can be. Measured by completed tasks in all aspects of our lives. To do so in a way that benefits all that we can around us. To always leave things better than we found them and to be a positive energy in all we do and say.

When RRR is done correctly, the self-imposed distractions of self-doubt, self-pity and self-destruction of all types will just have to get in line as you Reset and clear them away. Then, you Refocus on your why and reasons for your direction and task and you are Recommitting to make it happen and go forward again, right on task. Soon, it will happen with ease. Those obstacles that were once in your way will become easier and easier to remove as distractions all together.

Plus, as you end each day with a note of gratitude, celebration, and a smile over the little wins, you will have habits of winning that will really drive the success to meet you in your journey. I have coined a direct reminder of this mental tool and habit for success of RRR247. Reset, Refocus, Recommit, 24 hours a day, 7 days a week. It is a mindset for success, using the mental tools of RRR all the time.

CHAPTER 13

YOU CANNOT RESET THE PAST, MOVE FORWARD

You cannot erase the past. You cannot travel back in time. You can, however, move forward. Control the things you can control. Live and learn. And, hopefully, progress. In this journey of life, we are seeking freedom. Freedom from anything that creates a binding grasp of our time, our income, and our ways of life to do whatever we want to do.

When you wallow or spend time regretting or reliving the past, it creates an expensive diversion in your path and journey to the success you deserve. It is also one of the most devious intruders to a mindset for success. We are all human; we all make mistakes, and we all seem to want to suffer and make sure we punish ourselves over and over for our wrongs.

In football, the Quarterbacks that make mistakes, get back up and go again on the next play are said to have a short-term memory. They forget the mistake and get back to doing their trained motions and executions. Beating yourself up over and over again for something that is already done, never helps you. It never works. It is getting over your mistake, past it and moving forward that gets it done. It is the RRR that allows you to get back onto focus and commitment to do, to achieve, and to win.

Mistakes and failures are the building blocks to an empire of success. They show you what not to do, and why. They become learning points to be better at being the better you. The quicker you can let go of the past, move on to learn from it and to become better, the quicker you can allow yourself to truly win.

We all make mistakes and horrible choices. I wish I could take back many of the decisions that I have made. I can also say with certainty that some of the biggest mistakes I have made turned out to be the best decisions; I just did not realize it until years later. Sometimes, the bad choices are not always bad. Sometimes, they are hard to understand until we look back at the path we are on and reflect on how we got there.

To error or to fail is also to discover a way that does not work for you. When speaking on the invention of the lightbulb, Edison said that "[he had] not failed. [He had] just found 10,000 ways that won't work." Sometimes, failure lets you see things from the correct angle or perspective. The Universe truly works in ways we do not always see or understand. Sometimes, we need to just pick ourselves up and continue the path we are on. Reset, Refocus, and Recommit are doing just that, regardless of it being small things, large things or especially those things that seem impossible to get through.

Failure and success are both ways to progress if you continue to keep going and learning from them. Success is always awesome, but failures often allow for the creation of multiple successes. Thrive on every single one. Just Reset, Refocus, Recommit, and keep getting up and going from each.

CHAPTER 14

GOLDEN RULE IS GOLDEN LIFE

Treating others, the way you would want to be treated is a perfect summary of this. However, there is far more to it than just the surface. And since it is becoming less and less passed down from families to their children, it is important to stress it wherever we can. Success is a universal right. It is the right of us all. However, it is also in coordination with us aiding in the success of others. It is in everything we do. Our basic actions throughout each day to our large impacts we can build towards.

This is something that should be a habit and part of your every action and thought. It isn't hard. In fact, it is easier than not doing it. The positivity and happiness that it creates flow into your everyday life.

The few rules I absolutely live by include:

- Do unto others as you would have others do unto you.
- Harm none. Seriously. Do not ever do anything with the intent to harm anyone.

- Leave things better than when you found them.
- Treat everyone in the manner that you would want to be treated. Do so as if you were in their shoes.
- Always look to serve others in any way you can. Through serving others we ourselves gain.
- Even the little things matter, and a smile does go a long way.
- Gentlemen do exist and need to act like it all the time. Open doors for others and always smile and be helpful and kind.
- Chivalry is not dead; it flows through all our DNA. When we take care of our neighbors there is always a strength that is felt by all around.

Good things do happen to good people. We must all be good and then realize we deserve the great things in life. Ask for it with a solid celebration of receiving the blessings. We get what we ask for and we are all entitled to be a part of the solution for everyone's success. Always remember we are meant to have an overabundance of life's rewards. There is far more than enough for everyone, and I mean globally. No one should be without. No one.

By connecting with this and going forward you will gain opportunities to help others. There is an incredible reward in all aspects of life when you connect with the universe and help others. One of my most incredible achievements is the creation of a system to aid and support anyone willing to be teachable so that they can grow and become better. It was not about short-term assistance, but lifetime assistance, allowing them to also become part of the solution on a global scope.

Not just creating a one-time solution but teaching others how to literally fish. Teach them a way to gain in a large way in order to help others. It is a pay it forward process that allows for anyone to help themselves and others. The more they help others, the more they gain. Incredible achievement, and one that I will continue as long as I am on this planet. It was put together following God given talents, decades of perfecting myself and my skills, and then taking the time to follow the few rules listed above to create a process, a system, and a way to make it run efficiently.

The more I put into making it happen, the more things fell into place. It was evident that the universe was not only on my side, but it was finding ways to bring the vision together for the solution that it needed to be. Saying that it is incredible is an understatement.

Never underestimate the good you can do by yourself. Find a way to pay it forward and watch the universe jump right in. We are truly a blessed and fortunate race of human beings here on earth.

CHAPTER 15

THE POWER OF MULTIPLE STREAMS OF INCOME

When it comes to this chapter, know that this topic is something I have known about since I was 14. It was something that just made absolute sense. There was no internet available in 1988. A lot of the things necessary for what was to come in my life were not yet available to me. Still, I just knew this was the way it was going to be done.

It was a truth I understood from early on, yet not until 2008 was it fully in scope to where I could share and teach it to others. It was something that others in the business world would discuss and throw out, usually with regards to real estate. It was a term that, again, sounded incredible but needed something more than will power to create. You needed to have systems, technology, and lead generation.

For me, it just seemed to make logical sense that multiple streams of income were my only method to truly get what I wanted and knew I was meant to have. It was also something I was directly involved in creating with my clients. While I was delivering the resources and technology to create these multiple streams of income, and working with more and more new millionaires each year, it was an understanding that began for me several years earlier. They say truth will always remain truth.

From the time I was eight years old, I have been making money by buying and selling things people wanted. I would buy in bulk and make profits in the mark up. I could get away with higher markups on certain products and some were breakeven but attracted the customer. Then, I would look for more things to sell the customer. Once the relationship was open, more things were easier to sell. These products were self-funded marketing. They brought customers through the door.

This began an instant understanding of the marketing house. I saw it with the stores my family went to. The local grocery store would keep competitive with the eggs, the milk, and the dairy. Other items would be more expensive, but people seemed to be emotional only about the basics. I watched as the local grocery became the baker, the butcher, and soon the home goods store all-in-one. Made sense to me. Getting customers into the door was the hardest part of the business. From there, it was all about offering them the solutions and products they needed for everything. I got it from the first time I realized the business direction of the marketplace happening right before us.

I was very head strong and bold as a child. I came from a family that could barely pay their bills from last month with what came in this month, or even two or three months out. Should a major appliance die, the devastation to the family required help from Grandpa and Grandma. Birthdays, holidays, and Christmas were horrible as compared to the neighbors or anyone else I knew. We were not homeless; we had each other, and luckily, we were healthy. There was a huge void, and it was not just income. It was all sorts of things. It was only satisfied when I was serving and helping others to become better.

I was often asked what I wanted to be when I grew up. It was comical, really. Aunts, uncles, and their significant others, as well as other adults around, asked me this question. They seemed to have a huge interest in my desires. They also came at me with amazing advice, advice from a point of no true knowledge. They were not millionaires, and by all regards not wealthy in financial means. They would ask me what I wanted to be, and I would say I was going to a millionaire, and wealthy. I wanted to be as far away as where I came from as possible.

I didn't want to go to the grocery store and worry about the budget; I didn't want to have to wonder if I had bought more than what I could afford. I remember so many times where my Mom had to put things back because we went over what she had a budget for. Admirable on one hand, but sad on the other. No one should have to do that. With all the many ways there was to make an income, no one should be without. They just need to know what to do.

The more things I found to sell to those that needed what I had, the more income I was bringing in. I was able to put food on the table to help feed my family from 12 years old on up. I could make the holidays and birthdays for my siblings' fun and rewarding, and I could buy what I needed to make life better. I was able to do this based upon doing several things depending upon the season and needs of the clientele I was building up.

For me, it was a matter of building up several things. If I wanted to make more than one million a year, I needed to hit $88k a month. I rounded it up to $100,000 a month. I was not seeing the path easily to this number by only doing one thing. Up to my 14th year of life, I had made money with multiple products and services. It seemed logical that 100 projects paying $1000 a month each would give me a solid path to $100,000 a month. I looked for ways I could do this without trading hours for income. I moved in and out of products and services that were related to my main focuses. This created habits and a vision that enabled today's success and the abilities to share them with countless others.

As technology and the internet created better means of delivering products and services to the masses, it became a perfect medium to deliver on my vision of multiple streams of income.

When I was in middle school, I was told by all around me that I should go to college and become a doctor or a lawyer. Everyone, that is, but my grandparents and parents. They seemed content with me being me, but for everyone else it was apparent that the board game of life was a great educational background. They seemed to really want to support my desire to become rich with advice that they themselves had not followed. For them, their solution was for me to become a lawyer or a doctor. No one suggested creating a business or sticking to the one thing I was naturally born good at: marketing.

They were my elders, and they were very adamant that their impressive suggestions were the path I needed to take. I had some interest in law, and it was incredible how my following their instruction towards a career in law made them leave me alone in my dream and desire to be a millionaire. I wanted so much more than to own the struggles my parents went through. I did not want to go without anything again.

Taking the study and learning advice from my Grandfather to actual results, I hit the library. I started studying medicine and law. I liked the intrigue of the medical side as well as the unresolved areas of research. I was not all that excited about the required schooling to be an expert or specialist in medical fields. It was in being a specialist that the millions were available. In law it was a clear path that criminal attorneys had the best odds at the millions. I knew that knowledge was everything in having the upper hand in any business, let alone in the legal profession. So, I did what I was taught to do, and I hit the library. Every single book on law was at my disposal. I read and consumed them all.

Granted, I was mostly interested in the fun of law that was presented through the black and white television show of Perry Mason. After diving into the mock trials, and a short internship with a criminal law firm, my desire to be in law was quickly killed. It all took place when I studied the statistics of what lawyers made, and what was required to work in the high paying aspects of criminal law.

I had learned that listening to advice, usually given freely and loudly by those that should not advise, was dangerous. I was interested in law, and I have been utilizing it often, only through attorneys that took the education and path I left to build as an entrepreneur around the globe.

I am so glad that I listened to those that had what I wanted. As I followed my path into marketing and sales, it took me into printing. Then, it took me from printing into computer telephony, where I was around a clientele that was making millions. They were both university educated and self-educated. They had multiple income streams, though they put a lot of focus into a main business model.

Being raised in a Military family, by a strong Marine, my upbringing was disciplined. I lived out of a footlocker and a cot for a bed until I turned 12. I still have that footlocker to this day and cannot for the life of me get rid of it. All being said the lessons and structure taught has played a great role in who I became.

I went forth and built-up telecommunication services and added multiple clients to build my wealth from. Each large account was access to $1000 or more a month. I added more and more accounts and built-up things for years. I was doing millions in business monthly, and by 2003 was ready to follow the way of all things technology and migrated from computer telephony to internet-based solutions.

I had already begun the direction to the Internet in 1994, and by 1997 I was all online and building. As things progressed, I was able to not only create multiple income streams, but to create a system that allowed more income streams to be plugged in to gain from work already being done to drive the people into the marketing house that was created. The very process was not just great for creating the sales from marketing properly, but it also created a way to market and add additional incomes.

From 2008 and on, it was a path that fulfilled my personal desire to help others and to follow the pathway the Universe and God had placed me on. Not only was I able to create multiple streams for my family and I, but I was able to duplicate the results and processes to create the results with others. I was also to learn from mistakes and perfect the system to where I could remove and replace anything with a better solution or product, and to do it in a way that didn't lose the marketing already in place.

Today, this is more available to those willing to learn the way of marketing with technology and the correct high touch necessary in the processes, systems, and programs we support. The processes and systems are incredible, and the available methods allowing success also work with our professional marketing and lead generation to target growth in our most successful areas within the marketplace we created. Basically, we took hard and made it easy, so anyone could do it.

For me, I honed in my skills and resources to provide a method of marketing that would work with anything and everything. The right things performed better, and the lesser things had places in the outskirts and indirect methods tied into the marketing platforms we utilize and build on.

I learned young that linear income was never a way to get where I wanted to go in wealth and accumulation. It was not hard to see it, not for me. Look at anyone working for a fixed income. For example, my Mother could only make so much, and was skilled in a way that was not duplicable by others.

Things are great until they are not. When their car breaks down, the dryer dies, or the furnace goes out, they are behind the bills and seemingly never get back. Cost of living only increases, and the income you receive in a linear fashion can never keep up. There are only 24 hours in the day. Something must happen where you are earning income from things that are not a trade for time. The odds of inventing something or winning the lottery are so slim that it is hardly worth talking about. Enter into a world of marketing where there is more need for marketing than there are people to ever make it happen. Now, you have found the one area that anyone can become a part of and have access to creating an income, if not several incomes.

Think about it. Marketing is freedom, freedom we all deserve. The more we all understand and take part in marketing, the more freedom we have access too. Wow, right?

I have never been unemployed and other than one eight-month period in my life I have never been employed. That eight months I poured my heart, soul, and God given talents to increase the sales and income of the store I was working at. When I proved my worth and asked for a raise, I was told by the store manager that there was nothing he could do. I was told that if I stayed around until I turned 18, that I could become an assistant manager. I did receive access to receive free products in lieu of a raise to keep me around. He had received trips and awards in the time I was there because of the increases in sales. It was then that I realized the employer to employee structure was not a structure I wanted to live with. It became clear that, for me, any job without room for marketing and sales compensation was not for me, and I immediately knew then what to look for before trading my time for money again. I never even did that again. I went into marketing and sales driven income fully from that point forward.

I can tell anyone that a knowledge and understanding in marketing is vital to never being out of work ever. Want freedom? Marketing is the key to freedom for anyone. Marketing makes the world go around. Religion, or even Cocaine, does not sell on its own. Marketing is freedom.

For those that have an income from being employed, that is a great start. You still have time outside of that to pursue an additional income, or to get into a system that creates several incomes at the same time. Education is where it begins. Understanding the way of marketing forever allows you to fish in the world. Application is where the fun is.

Having a stable set monthly income is a great starting point; consider it a foundation to build from. As you see the vertical income increasing, you can, at the right point, say goodbye to the linear income and get back that precious time. Build yourself into true time and financial freedom.

The internet made the options of successfully marketing a product for profit a reality for literally millions of people. However, there is always room for more. There is an incredible law of marketing that everyone should realize. It is so true, yet I have seen many businesses, corporations, and even large technology firms act as if it does not exist. I have frankly heard the most incredible affirmation of this law of marketing by one company out of Utah that they really spun my head. They built up a hype about a digital product that had not even launched yet. They were incredibly cocky and full of themselves. They did something that even the largest companies of the world have yet to ever do. They claimed that they were launching with all the marketers they would ever need. Ever. They said they needed no additional marketing, and they had all they needed to grow their business forever. They delayed launch; they finally launched; they had initial sales from their hype; and then they plummeted. By the time they went after new marketing partners, they were an even larger joke in the industry. They clearly, amongst other things, did not understand this law. The law of marketing.

I am going to be more than clear to anyone right here: it does not need to be believed by you, but it is a law. It is the truth to the power of what marketing truly is. No matter how great your new product or service is, it will not sell itself. Just as true as the law of gravity, where, regardless of your belief in it or not, should you jump off the roof of your house, you will come crashing down and probably will break your leg. The law of marketing is incredibly vital to any and every business. The lack of marketing is the main reason any product or service fails to reach the public. A lack of marketing is the number one reason any business fails. A lack of marketing is a lack of clients, and therefore a lack of revenue.

The worst products with the best marketing can succeed in spite of their product because of marketing. Connecting a product or service with a consumer is the key goal. The products we market can pay a commission on a one-time basis, or, in the situations I focus on, every time they are purchased by the same client.

Utilizing the tools of web systems, marketing systems, and tools, we can market and promote all categories of products and services. Each of these represent an income stream. The more products we categorize and make easy to market, promote, and get in front of the consumers, the more streams of income we are working with.

The marketing systems we utilize in this internet filled world, one that we are seeing develop every day, is virtually never ending. As more innovations are discovered, invented, and presented to us, there are more income streams we can add to our marketing solutions already in motion.

This is the most incredible opportunity for anyone that is willing to learn, and it is all about marketing and working smart. Utilizing technologies, systems, and guidance from proven use of the tools and systems to gain and create incomes, we can gain multiple streams of income.

Look at it from a supermarket standpoint: every product they carry represents an Income stream; the more they offer, the more income streams they can create. Every time a customer enters the store, they can make incomes. This repeats for them every time that customer comes back as well.

When was the last time you saw a grocery store close its doors? When you build with the right systems and the right trends, you can create the same results. Leverage time, innovations, and systems to maximize what you can make in multiple streams of income. Take advantage of income for actions instead of income for your set time each day. Then, make it happen for more things within the same structure that you are part of. It sounds hard, and it is hard until you gain the right mentoring, the right training, and access to the right technology to make it easy. Then, anyone can do it.

SECTION III

ENGINEERING AN INCREDIBLE FUTURE FOR ALL

CHAPTER 16

THE CHANGING WORLD AND WHAT IT MEANS TO YOU

Change is constant, change is always happening. The universe wants us to succeed. It wants us to grow. It is an unstoppable force. With these changes comes innovations. Some ways of life become changed or lost along the way. Other ways of adapting and creating a new way to do things are always being created. It is a true evolution that has been happening from the start of mankind.

We all know that change is constant. We need to learn to not panic with change. We are humans and we have and always will adapt. With adaptation comes opportunity. The end of something creates the beginning of something else. Because of this, there are more ways today than ever to adapt with change, and in doing so create more ways to share the wealth and prosperity around the globe. The tools and systems available today make success so much more attainable. The creation and adaptation of work from home jobs, careers and self-employment opportunities has never been as available as they are today. And this has been a trending growth area for decades. And it is only going to become more and more common.

The sheer technologies today in communications and management tools allow us to command our workforce regardless of their location. Accountability is visible and reporting tools allow you to manage all aspects of your operation effectively from anywhere. Our home offices today turn into solid workplaces. And we will see a trend of increased expenses in home remodeling to allow for full time living and working within the same space. Designs in new homes will be heavily focused on work and living space and how they work together. This is also another example of adapting to the changes. This then leads to the creation of more opportunities in design and solutions for the needs of better home office space and utilization.

Today we have thousands of partners that tie into our phone and support systems to build incomes around the globe. The days of large office space for us is no longer a need. This is becoming the same situation for small, medium, and large firms.

We have created ways of ecommerce and business success that is accomplished through teams. And we are creating incomes to be shared with many. All because of the marketing success we have and share in a growing environment ready to add others as fast as possible. Where the growth and opportunities are virtually without limits. We have and will continue to spread the education and training to the ever-evolving world around us. And in doing so allow for more wealth distribution to help end poverty and to help create a better quality of life for all we can.

Logistics companies have created solutions to where same day, next day, or within a few days we can purchase and have delivered just about anything to our front door. The ease and comforts provided by the thriving businesses of today are changing the way the consumer purchases and experiences the entire buying process.

And no matter the evolution of these services and constantly evolving ways we interact with each other, marketing will always be a need. The law of marketing truly makes marketing the solution to freedom.

Following the law of marketing is truly like teaching a man to fish, and if you know how to fish, you can always feed yourself and your family. Because of the internet, the marketing systems, and the knowledge to use them, you can be a successful marketer from anywhere in the world that you have a functioning device and the internet. Never has the true freedom made available by this been as great as it is. And it is only getting better and better. Again, marketing is freedom.

CHAPTER 17

THE FAMILY ECONOMY

Sadly, many do not learn the basics of economics, not even at a small personal or family level. When it comes to the family economy, I am blown away at the lack of understanding that most have in this regard. So, let us start out by saying that your family, be it a family of one or a family of 11 (or more), is a family unit. Remove the emotions, they do not pay you, and they only cost money. Focus on the logic, and the moving pieces that create the family economy.

For my family, members were tied into the family businesses from the time they could operate and understand. For most of them that age was eight. They were given tablets, laptops, gaming machines, smart phones, etc. as soon as they were able to begin to understand.

We have been blessed and we have been part of marketing solutions and income streams (multiple) for decades now. With these blessings we have been able to create a lifestyle that has allowed us to travel together often. The children were able to participate and as they became older, they were able to be more involved.

The projects and work we do preferably create an ongoing residual income. This is something that we prefer. We do the heavy lifting and solve the largest need for most any business, getting clients. This creates income. Great. Now on the other side of the coin is the outgoing expenses. Earnings or income, and costs or expenses. Just like a business (or rather, it is a business). This is the family economy. Regardless of self-employment income or income from an employer, it is income. And regardless of income we all have the expenses of life. Rent or mortgage, housing costs. electricity, gas, oil, solar, utilities, water, sewer. Then groceries, right? Household needs for cleaning, sanitizing, and maintaining a residence. Clothing, furnishings, dry cleaning, and other needs around these categories. Self-care and hygiene products. All of these things. Then you have transportation, cars, trucks, fuel, and maintenance of our transportation vehicles. All of these things. You should be getting the picture. If it is not documented, it is out of control. Guessing or flying by the seat of your pants is adding the emotion of crazy to your life. And I promise you it is awfully expensive.

The knowledge of your net Income is crucial. This is the overall income you bring in on a weekly or monthly basis. This is the income to your family economy. It is what you have to create a life with. It is your funds for covering the roof over your head, the clothing on your back, the food in your belly and the means to continue it all.

Then it is the knowledge of your monthly expenses. When you have more expenses than income, this is a deficit. One that usually piles up on credit cards and loans. Something that can create so many issues, problems and even a disaster within the family economy. This can lead to bankruptcy or devastating income issues, the most common reason of divorce and issues within a marriage. Pretty crazy if you ask me. Saw it happen with my own parents and countless others. I mean there are enough issues in life without adding financial issues and stresses to it. No one needs financial stress. And after you read this book, I am telling you the solution and creation of freedom is marketing. And no matter how much anyone says they do not like to sell things; nothing is as bad as financial issues. And be careful, when you learn the true ways of marketing, you will probably like it more than you ever realized:

"Marketing done properly makes sales become order taking."
- Rory Ricord.

Now, I will add in some helpful things that my wife, Tanya, and I do. We discuss family economics together, in the evening, always over a glass of wine. It is usually something red, a Merlot or Cabernet Sauvignon or Pinot Noir. We toast and celebrate our life and blessings and then drink. Then we go about it and evaluate and adjust.

We could absolutely do better. Meaning we could hold ourselves to a budget for our expenses and lifestyle. Both of us grew up in families that budgeted. Tanya was 1 of 10 children in her family, I was 1 of 5. Tanya and I have seven children together and we have been able to provide for their every need and want. We wanted more for our children than we had ourselves, and we both had issues with budgets when it came to basics. Not problems sticking to a budget, but in remembering the pains they represented in a life of being broke.

We just work smarter, harder and with more focus. To us the reward was so we could have and eat and do what we wanted. We could live. We could play. And for us it works, but again, we are bringing in far more income than we need for expenses. I can tell you that if something drastic or unexpected were to happen, we both would clamp down in all areas we could and figure it out. That is because we have the habits and at the same time, we enjoy life. Today, tomorrow, and always. We make it that way. Why? Because we learned the power and magic of marketing. Again, marketing is freedom.

For most everyone that is not to where we are yet, we get it. We teach and help in the same ways we would go about it. With budgets. The rewards of creating your deserved over-abundance in income and wealth is that you get to do more, experience more, and the issues that are made big by small-minded (or broke-minded) habits no longer apply to you.

Budgets are temporary and dangerous. They are a way of manifesting to the universe that you only need so much, that you want to go against the natural course of overabundance. This is a concept that even my best students have a hard time with, and it really is as simple as it sounds. The reality is that most that come into our training are already behind and upside down. They are living on credit because they emotionally made decisions and are paying the price of interest.

Now this is where the family economy needs to become clear. When you are looking to create more income for your family, you need to realize that there is a fundamental approach to creating income. In almost every aspect of income creation, there is a cost to the business. It truly takes money to make money.

The family economy has expenses. Some of them were placed on credit cards along the way. Some are business or income costs that allow the income to be created. For example: clothing for the job; the labor being done; the car, gas, and maintenance to allow you to get to and from the job. These are all things you need to succeed and be able to make an income.

We have broke-minded people that come into our training program. They spend money on things that are emotional purchases. They do not make money from these items, and yet, they financed the purchases in order to get them immediately instead of when they could afford them. They are willing to go into a financial hole for these items, yet when an opportunity that they seek out has a cost to it, they literally freak out. It is education, understanding and environment. They have never been shown the very concepts I have covered in this book.

You will never find a successful business or businessperson that has ever had success without investing time and money--both time and money. Even a job requires initial investment in clothing and needs before ever generating a paycheck. Once you invest into something, you will take it more seriously because you need to create income from it to make it worthwhile. If you put your time or money into something, you better back it up with your best. Decide what you want to get done, then act accordingly.

There is also something more to work on and understand. As you create the income streams, you want to be sure to pay off the interest accumulating accounts and get your family economy to be more and more debt free. There are fundamentals that occur in the family economy that can allow for wealth accumulation. It is something you need to turn into more of a business in how you treat it. Treat it like a business, and you will find that the decisions you make will become easier and less emotional. The family economy can only become profitable and grow profits when it is focused like a business.

You will need to reinvest into the business over and over again. The more you learn and gain, the hard will become easy. Often, I have shook my head at the quitting mentality of an employee-minded person. They will complain that building a business takes investment and reinvestment over and over again to build it to profits. They will see this as an issue yet will have no problem investing their precious time repeatedly for years or even decades in a dead-end job or dead-end occupation. Success has no room for quitting. And quitting has no business being in your activities for succeeding. Ever.

CHAPTER 18

WHEN THE FAMILY ECONOMY TAKES ON SYSTEMS OF FREE ENTERPRISE

Depending on how serious you build your income streams, your income needs, and your expenses can turn into an incredible thing to your favor. See as you tap into multiple streams of income and the success is created; it is time to build upon it. Free enterprise is going to kick in at some point and your decisions on how you spend your time and money will change. Meaning, freedoms in time and money will be created.

My goals with each of my students is to get them to where their time freedom becomes one of the most incredible choices to make. At some point the incomes coming in from a system allowing multiple streams of income creates some incredible life choices. Mom and dad can both work from the home. Time spent building the vertical incomes will surpass anything linear. There is no way the pressure and craziness at the job can compare to the true freedoms of time and money that vertical incomes create. And yet again, marketing is freedom.

Free enterprise kicks in. The ability to make more and more money for the same time, energy invested in can become something truly incredible.

Yet it is the same principle of any successful business. The ability to scale income as compared to costs of business. Now you decide where your time is best spent. You have freedoms to choose your aspects of life. All of them.

The goal of what I have been part of creating is to create an understanding of where the family can go into the future. The more we see the changing landscape of the globe with the Internet and the marketing systems the brighter the future is. Sharing the knowledge with our family can allow us to pass on the income streams and the knowledge to create more (an over-abundance) for our children and their children.

The new products and services only need to be plugged in. The environment of success and the ability to access it from anywhere with internet access required means we can live and operate anywhere. No more are boundaries set to any one location. This is the freedom that marketing, and the use of it with systems and the internet, provides.

CHAPTER 19

BENEFITTING FROM A FAMILY OF "FAMILY ECONOMIES" ALL USING "SYSTEM OF FREE ENTERPRISE."

Depending on how you are understanding what I am saying within these pages, life can become more and more free. For all that, jump on the education, understanding and application of marketing. With marketing and the opportunities, it is constantly creating endless possibilities. Marketing is freedom after all.

The family unit can not only thrive; but it can become an ever-growing environment to promote and guide the next generations to greatness and boundaries where financial concerns are no longer a barrier. New wealth is created all the time. Regardless of your background and understanding before, the new futures of today and tomorrow become incredible.

We see this as we work with thousands and thousands of new students. We get so close to our students as we grow together and share in the freedoms available from the marketing and success available. Marketing is the ever-expanding need to make the world go around! There is something about it. It is the everything that makes things work.

Nothing has ever been so incredible to share and develop the family economy as marketing and the available rewards and true freedom it creates.

See, there is a hard and true part of marketing that can never be fully automated. This is why marketing will always be something that anyone can make a living with. The needs to run a family can be created and successful with so much less success than in times before.

There are hard ways to do things, sure. There are also ways that have been proven by those that understand it and better, understand the ways of the universe. Paying it forward and sharing with many, not few is where the truth in happiness lies.

Having the knowledge and understanding is one thing. Being able to share it with others, to allow them the success and happiness and true freedom from it is another.

When you understand and are applying this to your family, there is the next step. Taking it to share with other families. As you do this, the power of combined "families" working to build, growing together is incredible. Creating a community around the ideals and solutions created grows.

The incredible power of working together can overcome the hardest of obstacles. And it is an incredible bond to grow, learn and achieve together. Building and growing as partners and a community allows for so much more in shared results and growth. Especially when you are like minded and doing things in the manner to which is right. Incredible things happen in the family unit and in a community, it is even stronger.

If you can create an environment that not only helps others but does it in a community setting, it will allow for the strength in numbers to help everyone even more. We are better united in all things. We were never meant to do anything alone.

CHAPTER 20

COMMUNITY STRENGTH IN NUMBERS

As an extrovert, I thrive on the company of another, and even more with the company of several others. As I have been covering in the chapters within this book, succeeding by yourself is one thing, I know it well, however, nothing is as rewarding as helping others to succeed.

When we decided in 2008 to take the marketing solutions that we discovered in the previous decades with others, we knew it was our true calling in life. The thing about it, though, was we wanted to find a way to help those that truly needed it.

We knew that this would be a challenge. Why? Traditionally the rich get richer and the poor get poorer. It's simple. We are 90% a product of our environment. This means that if we come from parents that are employees, we most likely are, or will be, employees ourselves. If we have parents that are business owners, then odds are we too are, or will be, business owners.

Financially stable families pass on the knowledge and environment of success that they have had with their children. Those with poor and humble environments pass on what they know. It is only when someone seeks a change to their environment that they allow for change to happen.

My wife and I both did not come from wealth, but we have had some incredible self-made family successes. Thanks to the life choices we made, and our desire to have much more than we had, we were open to learning and gaining from the mentoring of others.

There is no way we could take the blessings of life and not become the vessels of solutions for so many that did not come from an environment of prosperity. It has created a true understanding of why people cannot get ahead. Yet, in our lifetime, the internet and the free flowing of knowledge and information was no longer bound by books. It was available easily and freely. Oh, and we are "professional marketers."

God did not give me the talents and opportunities that he gave me just to benefit me and myself. Can you imagine the reckoning if we wasted our blessings because we did not pay it forward? I can, and it is enough to fire me up to do as much as I can for others all the time, every day. Not everyone is the same. We all have different talents, understandings, and everything else. We are unique. All of us.

This is where the marketing we tapped into becomes so powerful. Sure, we can all follow the same duplication systems for marketing, but the actual available opportunity for each and every one we share it with, is there, because we are unique. Our uniqueness is valuable in the very nature of our work within the opportunity. It is incredible. So much so it is natural.

I have been at the marketing process to sell services and products for as long as I can remember. I have made income since I was eight years old, and I did not stop, ever. Once I got a taste for the income and what it could provide, I had my path. I have also been doing something I genuinely enjoy for a very long time. I do not consider it work. I get to do something that creates pleasure and fun for me each and every minute of each and every day. I have been able to share this with so many others, and yet my work is never done.

You know, I have always been a person that gets frustrated when I cannot create a solution to a problem. I know more than most that we cannot control everything, and we can only fix those things to which we do control.

Obvious, yeah, but it is deeper than that. I have been trained to be solution oriented, and I have also been a part of some incredible solutions. To solve something is to be of huge value, and usually this is worth being compensated for.

Marketing is the literal solution to the largest issues in any business. Without marketing, the business will die. Period. It is simple math. If you do not have consumers to buy your product or service, then you cannot run a business. There are expenses to just being in business, and if you do not bring in income, you will eventually be out of cash to even exist as a business. Harsh reality, right?

Marketing is the changing point of any business. Even a mediocre product or service can thrive with the proper marketing behind it. Believe me, I have been a part of solving all sorts of issues over the past decades. As the lead king and the marketing magician, I have changed the outcome for many businesses. Sales, and the revenues from the sales, fix everything.

I watched as our society made both parents of a family work. I watched how the destruction of the strong family unit became a sad reality. The issues in society become larger, and all of them, in my solid mind of reason, were related to the lack of a mom and a dad in the home to raise and develop the future, the children. Here, we were raising our children together from home. We were able to volunteer daily in their schools, and to keep up with them and their friends all the time. We have been so blessed.

We had something that others were not knowledgeable about, right? We could do it, and here is the kicker, you ready? We were professional marketers. I mean, we were marketing things for our clients. Why not market and bring in people that needed what we had? Why not teach and share with them in a manner that would help fix the issues of our society, one family at a time?

Even the best ideas and solutions are nothing if they are not marketed. We had the solution, we built the training platform, and we had the God given gifts and solutions to market anything, so we did.

In 2005, I ran into some issues doing online marketing with Google and their search engine rules. These issues needed a solution. This solution would prove to be something incredible, something that would create the need for millions of marketing partners: the ability to share our training and methods to market, which would allow the strength of numbers to beat out the competition of the largest of companies. No one could compete with us.

Starting in 2008, we began to grow this solution with every new student we added to our system. This is something that is truly above and beyond the normal reach of anyone else. It was extremely hard at first—I'm not even exaggerating. I knew it was do or die. We were solid. We had been so blessed and secured by the graces of God, and the successes coming at us. We had to do it. I knew it would work; it did and does.

Thousands are building their family economies, and more are helping us to pay it forward to others. The world will forever be changing from this motion of sharing and paying it forward. More families will be benefiting from this than ever.

We created a method that, the more it is done, the more successful it is. There is not a limitation. There is no saturation point. It is all about overabundance, and the vehicle to get there is only better when more people are involved. Everything that was discovered in my life and along this path are, all together, a perfect solution for all that want it for themselves and their families. It is the direction of the future. It is affecting the lives and family economies of many around the globe. There is no end. It is forever a direction.

The strength in the numbers of students, and what we call "partners," that we share these solutions with truly are without end. This marketing that we teach and participate in creates true freedom.

There is not freedom in anything where your time is traded for money. The very instance of needing permission from anyone about the time you have, and use is not freedom. Asking someone for permission to get time off to do something other than work is absolute slavery with payment. Sure, you get paid for being an employee or cog in the system of business that your employer has. I could tell you that if I had to ask permission to just do whatever I wanted to do, and if someone else controlled my time, I would lose my temper.

I do not need to participate in anyone's business based on their time needs from me to have an incredible life. Utilizing the systems and marketing tools I have been blessed with over these past decades, there is so much to gain, so much so that very few jobs could give me the financial and time freedoms that I have. I am unemployable, and I am on a mission to share this lifestyle with everyone I can. Millions can benefit from this.

There are parts of the world where $200 USD can create a great lifestyle. The internet allows them to participate in all that we do. We have the means to create hundreds of dollars in an hour. Some of us already do more than that, and there are almost no limitations to the incomes we can create every single day. It is not based upon the hour, but the action. The more actions we take, the more we can earn. Incredible possibilities.

We have something so incredible, and it becomes larger as we add more to it. The strength in our numbers only grows. The success we create, and make available, only increases by our size as well.

This is the fun of creating a solution in marketing that can be shared with anyone that becomes a part of it. Having the vision is one thing but having the system to support it is another. Then, the proven marketing solutions make it happen.

CHAPTER 21

THE BLESSING OF PAYING IT FORWARD

From an attitude of awesomeness to being part of true happiness, paying it forward is the absolute vehicle for it all. I am so serious right now. There is no true happiness as the happiness realized by helping others to achieve freedom. Time and money freedom. Freedom to live and work from anywhere. Freedom to raise their children exactly the way they want too. Money itself does not provide happiness. But the use of money to help others surely creates incredible happiness.

Solving the problems of the world is all about the freedoms available to the family unit. Solve that and the world will only become more and more amazing. Never before has this possibility been so available. Technologies only improve this possibility. Making it more available by the day. New ideas and technologies are being developed and introduced all the time. Being aware and ready to take advantage of them is the key.

Here we are. It is all here. It is all available. Just need to understand the principles and the needs to put in place to make it available for success for you and others you share it with. You need to allow your environment to change.

The universe works in incredible ways. We are all vessels of the magic it creates nonstop. The power within the universe creates life, creates successes, and creates the manifestations to make things happen in larger and larger ways.

The incredible power of the universe and the higher power within it are all about greatness. The truth of our purpose here on earth is everything to do with how and what we do to our fellow human beings.

When you feel down and out, help someone, serve someone. The natural reaction you feel is far more than almost anything for feeling good or great even. Service to others is where the best moments of self-worth and happiness are created.

My grandfather was always about the service of others. I can tell you that I helped others as a child constantly, because of his example. Often, with silence and stealth. The joy and happiness it gives me is always worthwhile. I still serve others; it is a habit, like breathing. Service is the best drug I have ever found. When you go and help out anyone without a hidden agenda of payment, the joy and happiness is incredible. I would have daily goals of how many I could help each day. It became a habit, and way of living.

The energy I have and live with constantly is an overabundance. I am in service to others on the daily. Also, I am happy all the time on a daily basis. I am told that it is almost sickening. Yet, it is my normal. It is how I will always be. It is an incredible feeling and something I never want to be without.

Sharing this feeling and ongoing blessing that comes from the universe because of it is even more enjoyable. There is no such thing as too much happiness. There are only incredible smiles, incredible energy, and happiness. This is a freedom from sadness or discomfort of being upset.

When I see the students learning and succeeding and then following in the path of giving back, it is so incredible. It is a new level of happiness. They are feeling it as they help others. The pay it forward is now in another generation of helping others.

This is only going to allow the passing on of the blessing and the helping of others to multiplication to others. I can only help one at a time. Sure, there are systems in place to help them along the way, but it is still a limitation. When you can help on a personal level, it then expands. If you can get it to continue to the next person from them and so on, well it can expand from 1 to 10 to 100 to 1000 to 10000 to 100000 and beyond.

Now, tie in economic models to reward this action with income and partnerships, and you are onto something that can create ways to help so many. No more relying on the job of old. Employer to employee relationships of old cannot hold a candle to what is possible with a process to help others without limits. Incomes no longer measured by the hour, but by the action. Actions now have virtually no limitations as they grow with the marketing systems. And if marketing is freedom, marketing systems are truly freedom-creating systems.

CHAPTER 22

TAKE ACTION. WHERE TO BEGIN.

For me, I have done things in the manner that was clear to me. This was often the opposite of what others would tell me or direct me. Granted, these "others" were teachers, business colleagues, family, and well-intended individuals. Many of which did not have or succeed in the manner of which I was seeking.

I have always solved marketing first. Then, I would solve for the demand that the marketing created. It is the habit to which my brain thinks and drives to any and all projects or opportunities with. If I cannot solve the marketing, then the project or opportunity really does not matter.

From my perspective, with almost everyone else, they would come up with an idea or a product and then decide to figure out the marketing. Many treat marketing with little respect. They come up with an idea for a product, or a way to improve a product or service already in use. It is something they taught in school even. Look to create a better mousetrap. How can you improve on an existing idea or product out in the marketplace already? Maybe this sounds like a wonderful idea to you. For me, there is that law of marketing. It is something that I've seen forgotten by large companies, startups and even projects with grand ideas. I realize this is repetition, but of all things to learn, the law of marketing is the biggest thing to take away from this book.

"Repetition is the mother of all learning."
- Fred Lake

There is another law I will use for an example to help explain this concept. The law of gravity. As we all know the law of gravity states that what goes up, must come down. It is a law. And whether you believe it or do not believe it, if you jump off your house you will fall. You will probably hit the ground hard and you will probably break your leg.

The law of marketing states that regardless of the product or service you are offering, if you do not have a method to market it, it will not sell itself. You could have the best product or service or even an okay product or service. Whomever has a method to market and share it with those who need your product or service will win. Even a less superior product will outperform in success when marketing is applied properly. It is also marketing that drives the levels of Success. Without marketing, anything will fail. And with marketing, the world goes around.

Religion does not sell itself. And on the other side of the coin (as I enjoy saying), Cocaine does not sell itself either. If you solve marketing first, and then find a product or service to connect to the methods of marketing; success has always been easier. Just wait until you get a grasp of the marketing lessons you are about to read. Marketers get to have all the fun. And, in today's digital age, where cookies and tracking have nothing to do with baked goods and wilderness, you are about to see the world in an entirely new perspective.

Where you begin is in marketing and the understanding of marketing in today's world. Solve your understanding of marketing first, then take action and apply it to better your life, your time, and financial freedoms, and to the betterment of others.

For me, the pleasure of sharing my life's passion, my life's work, and the many blessings I have received because of it all; this book was a place for me to take action. A place to begin. Each day I wake up, I get to help change and better the lives of those we as a community share. My work is never done and there are so many more to share these blessings with.

Just wait till I get to share more with you in the coming pages. Take it in and take action and begin a better life. You alone can make changes to better your life and then the lives of others. You choose when you take action. You choose where you take action. At home, at the office, in the fields of labor and in your community.

Let us begin with Marketing 101. We have shared in understanding, concepts and roads of education that open the mind for more. What is all that understanding without a path to express it all?

SECTION IV

RORY'S MARKETING 101 CLASS BEGINS HERE

CHAPTER 23

ASCENSION MARKETING AND THE PATIENT PROCESS

Okay, I am going to tell you something right here and now that I feel is important. We are going into something that makes me happier than most everything in this world. Well, other than my grandkids. My entire life has been the study of ascension: understanding my fellow man and the cunning of man; what makes us do the things we do, and why we do them; what are the actions we take, and why do we take them. We are emotional creatures, us humans. Literally speaking, without these emotions we would not get up in the morning. Without the emotions we have there would be no purpose or drive for what we do out of need and want.

No one just wakes up wanting to buy something that they see for the first time, nor does anyone make a decision on an initial introduction. Even when it is something that will enhance or better their life, they just do not do it. There is a process. We all buy and consume in this very process, so much so that it is not realized by the consumer. It is like breathing, inhaling, feeding our veins with oxygen and exhaling carbon dioxide. It is an important process that keeps us alive, but we do it so casually we only realize how important it is when we struggle with it. Consuming, and buying products and services, is just like breathing.

Combining the knowledge of ascension in marketing, and all of life's decisions, will help you understand more, and it will help you to be a better person. Apply that, along with the patience process, and we take a marketing understanding that allows us to be able to enhance almost every area of life.

Ascension is, by definition, to ascend. In life, in understanding, and in knowledge, it is rising up from level to level. When applied to marketing, it is educating and impressing on your clients, or future clients, to ensure you gain their buying actions in a later time. This is a deep understanding of our fellow men, women, children and even our elders. It is moved along in one of many patient processes. The patient process is incredible. To know it and apply it will allow any business to succeed in ways that they would not have before. It has to do with understanding your client or customer's needs in anticipation.

We will go into more with ascension marketing as it is part of all other marketing processes, systems, and psychological understandings. It is something that people who quit in any marketing related process, business, or action, truly need to understand. The process is not quick. It is hard, and it only becomes easy with repetition and sticking to a plan.

If you want to look at being successful, you can always look at those that have succeeded before you. Look around. The businesses that are successful are doing things that work. McDonald's, Walmart, and Target all market in many ways and all the time. They never stop. McDonald's spends millions a day on marketing. They lose market share and revenues when they lay off the gas to their marketing engines. They market in different ways, and with different strategies all running at the same time. They are involved in community outreach and awareness and they are constantly marketing.

This isn't just ascension marketing for today's business, but for tomorrow and the future. This is where it becomes incredible. See, there are two types of understanding when it comes to marketing and building towards the future. Not all understand the power of ascension marketing the same.

Let's take Ford and Chevy and compare them to Buick and Oldsmobile as examples for ascension marketing. Ford and Chevy have always been going at each other in competition. They have been at this game for so long that they really have done well playing off of each other. Buick and Oldsmobile are both in another category all together, and it is in the category of being losers in the measurement of time. Time is more expensive than you can realize until it is truly too late. Time is something we all have only so much of, and eventually we all leave this planet and run out of time. We are not forever clients.

Starting as far back as I could research, advertising and product placement, as long as there was a Sears catalog, there was branding, and ascension marketing being done by Ford. Chevrolet was right there too. Ford really got it, though, and I am certain that they were at it before Chevrolet. Although, Chevrolet was always right there following and working to one up Ford. This is healthy competition and is the reason that they have continued to improve things. They built up market share and invested heavily into the future. They understood their message and their loyalty and more importantly how to keep it. They may have the longest collection of data of any American company that I could look back at and study.

In the process of doing their marketing, Ford, and Chevrolet both went big on the future. They began branding to their clients decades before they were to become actual clients. I can tell you personally that it had such a strong effect on me that, even today, I am a Ford client; I have purchased 20 plus Ford vehicles and will continue to do so in the future. As my Grandfather did, I will be passing my loyalty and proof of it down to my children, and to their children, and so on. It all started before I was out of diapers.

See, Ford, and Chevrolet were placed within our grasp and shared with us from the earliest of moments. We saw their commercials during our cartoons and shows. We were given toys that were replicas of the latest and greatest Ford and Chevrolet vehicles. It was everywhere. And our uncles and elders would participate. Giving us models to build and toys to play with that were from their favorites. This was not just a toy thing, it was marketing; a ploy to get us to fall in love with Ford and Chevrolet. So that, as we got older the happy times we remembered with the toys and seeing the loyalty our elders had to the companies, when the time was right, would lead us to buy a Ford or Chevrolet for ourselves.

Meanwhile, following traditionalist thinking of loyalty for today's clients, Buick and Oldsmobile focused on their clients and kept them happy. They created programs and incentives to keep them coming back. Their focus was on their current clients. This was great, though it created a belief and understanding for the youth that it was for the older generations. They were not driving around a toy Oldsmobile or Buick. They were developing as future clients with Fords, Chevrolet's and being ascension marketed to constantly. The impressions of Ford and Chevrolet literally was driving them to their brand over and above all others. As the best. As the one they should have. Tying the joys of childhood with their driving vehicles in later life.

The costs of not participating in ascension marketing long term now has Oldsmobile and Buick playing against their choices of old. They literally market as "Not your Grandpa's Oldsmobile". They have time against them, and they have proof in the lack of market share across almost all the sectors to prove it.

Now today, mind you, it is proven, and you will see that almost every car and truck manufacturer are playing in the same marketing spaces. They have increased their product placements to be in movies, in television series and everywhere they can to keep us tied in. They will be all doing this more and more and it is a win-win situation for the consumers as well. Innovations and creating the better vehicle going forward is how we progress.

It is also a great way to learn and gain ideas for ascension marketing in your marketplace. With our students we set up multiple methods of ascension marketing from the get-go. It is something that does and will take time. It is an ongoing commitment to your business, your brand and to your long-term success.

We are in the world of social media and social proof results with clients. Competition is real and the more successful we become the more competition we can plan on running into. Doing even the smallest of marketing processes builds up. The more methods of ascension marketing the better.

Ascension marketing is also a byproduct of just being there. Those who stick around are the ones that get paid. There are factors that are going on. The trick is to have more methods of marketing going on and to stick to the processes and do everything to press on. There is a lot to gain with patience.

I have been told I have more patience than anyone has ever seen. The realization I came too years ago was that patience was something that would tie in with my successes. It is also a habit. There is a patient process to anything that is great. Again, it is where the hard becomes easy. Ascension marketing is doing the work and knowing that time is on our side. We are planting the seeds and letting the psychology of the marketing run its course. We are building the brand, the awareness and waiting for the client to realize the need for what we have.

The patient process is something that becomes a habit. You do not need to sit around idly either. Focus on what you can do and just let ascension marketing do what it does. Let it happen. Soon, when it starts to be effective it will look like things are just happening suddenly. They are really the rewards and outcome from the patient process that Ascension Marketing is creating and making happen.

You cannot rush the process it takes for ascension marketing to do what it does. You can understand it, support it and above all use it. Your competition, if they are smart, is using it too. Once you get it started, do not ever stop. It is a forever commitment to your success and ongoing success.

CHAPTER 24

COCA-COLA MARKETING

I already know this is clear to anyone that reads this. Why? Because, thanks to the actual truth of what I call Coca-Cola Marketing, you already know what Coca-Cola is. What you do not know probably is how and what Coca-Cola Marketing is. And believe me, it is simple, almost too simple. They found a way to teach everyone how to do it right. See Coca-Cola is everywhere. There is virtually no corner of the earth that you cannot find a Coca-Cola ad, billboard, sticker, and most importantly, their products.

At the core of Coca-Cola, they are not just a soda manufacturing company. WAIT, yes, I said that. They are a massive distribution company. They control the space on the retail stores and within restaurants all around the globe. They control the points of distribution to the customer. And from here they purchase brands and products to distribute through these points of distribution.

Coca-Cola controls several beverage and food items around the globe. They are something special though. To me, they are the best mass marketing organization on the planet. They have done things so well for a century now that are known by all. Even the third-world countries and their citizens know who and what Coca-Cola is. They know the brand and the product. And even the products next to Coca-Cola benefit from the awareness of their initial brand and product.

When I was an understudy of marketing with Squire International, a distributor of Coca-Cola in Utah, I was so awe-struck, and realized that marketing with them was a science of its own. I already saw the world from the eyes of a marketer. This was at an entire new level.

I am, and always will be, a guy that looks at the numbers and stats of anything. Math and numbers are the tell all of the results for anything. The issue with proper marketing is that measuring it is a long process. Ascension is a real thing. And it takes time. You need to measure and put out your expectations more than many realize or can understand.

It is not a one month or even a one-year scope of success and measurement. Oh no. It is decades. When I was with the Squire Executives and asking the questions that only I would, it was incredible. I was aware of the marketing agreements that Coca-Cola was making in many aspects. Pepsi was in the same regard, but for whatever reason, the Coca-Cola Distribution where Squire International was licensed, was dominating by double digits. They still are.

They literally set aside a marketing budget of $0.25 per can produced for distribution for marketing expenses. Knowing full and well that their return on that $0.25 per can was about 10 years down the road. This is marketing balls. Wow, the numbers allowed for this. No wonder as I traveled the globe and saw Coca-Cola ads and billboards and entire walkways covered in their colors and slogans were being displayed.

They take mass marketing to entirely new levels. And it is Coca-Cola globally. It is all by design and with complete purpose. They still do it today, and every day. They never stop. They are a mass marketing mega machine. And yet they are not just a cola or soda company. They occupy and control the retail spaces of convenience stores, grocery stores, restaurants, and venues all around the globe. They are incredible at what they do.

And they are giving and connected to the community. From youth programs to programs for the elderly. They do not publicize it; they just do it. Sponsoring the scoreboards and equipment for the youth programs all around the globe. Sure, there are offsets, where available, with their vending machine and ad placements.

They also dive into the marketing and sales psychologies that are proven, or even being proven. Incredible lessons in the ways to get noticed and into the minds of consumers. They are true pioneers and developers to ascension marketing. They are proof that advertising and a marketing plan is incredible together.

From making our happiest of moments connected with their products to having us think about them every time we are thirsty. Wow. They dominate our happiest of holidays. There is not a single person that cannot see Santa Claus without a Coke in his hand. The polar bears, the product placement in movies where Coke is always there. They are incredible innovators and pioneers in the ability to get us to see Coca-Cola, so much that we just go for it like a trained monkey. It is powerful and comes with knowledge and costs.

They have truly mastered several aspects of marketing. When I refer to anything as Coca-Cola Marketing it is a literal and utter call to respect. They have done something hard and made it so easy we honestly cannot recognize it. They have done it in a way that is easy to embrace and in a way that makes us happy.

When you look at what they have done and look around, you will see that they are first in almost anything done in mass marketing. Incredible. And with all that said, you will see that the mass marketing done in the beverage industry is following suite. And as much as you can sink into a cold glass of Coca-Cola or a Diet Coke, measure your happiness to a great glass of Pinot Grigio. Namely a Tanya Pinot Grigio. Yeah, it will be a bit more per glass, but so incredible.

With the law of awareness, you will be so much more aware of the Coca-Cola and their products being marketed around you. Subliminally, for your entire life really, it has always been there. It is reinforced non-stop.

Oh, and the Coca Cola merchandise and toys you have been seeing your entire life? That was also a long-term marketing process and tool of ascension marketing. Coca-Cola is ascension marketing from so many different aspects. And they are connected and intertwined with related products and services. From restaurants and amusement parks; sporting venues and televised events. They are everywhere they can possibly be.

CHAPTER 25

INDIRECT MARKETING

Indirect marketing is one of my favorite methods of marketing. I have probably made more income from it than from any other single avenue of marketing. We, as humans, buy on emotion. Things grab our attention, but we have a short attention span.

When we are shopping, looking, or poking around, we are in a trained state of consumerism. We have been trained to window shop, to browse, and to keep looking. It is a measured and controlled environment by the marketers amongst us.

Massive amounts of time, money, and resources are put towards perfecting indirect marketing. The results it creates are in every consumer sector out in the marketplaces, from the brick-and-mortar stores, to the online shopping experiences we are exposed to all around us.

This is where we are introduced to products, services, and items that we were not intending to purchase. We are introduced to these while we are in the process of consuming. It does not matter what we are looking to consume. Once we are in a location where we can consume and buy things, we are already dropping our guard and open to buying. So, the experience allows for accessories, or tag along items, to be put in front of us, or we get competitor products placed in front of us. Sometimes, it is just products that the statistics and sales numbers reflect are great products bought by similar consumers.

We have been conditioned by retailers and marketers for a long time now to buy more items than we originally intended to buy. We have been conditioned to expect upsells or to be shown even more things we can purchase when purchasing anything. Suggestions of things for us to buy even more at our time of purchase are at every check-out process both online and in retail stores. Even McDonald's has fashioned incredible profits from suggested additions to your order.

When we go looking for a particular item somewhere, and then get curious about a different direction altogether, that is indirect marketing. We will go in looking for a pair of shoes, and before you know it we will have two new outfits, and maybe we will have forgotten about the shoes all together.

Utilizing indirect marketing is all in technique and placement. Whether it is a retail storefront, or an online advertisement that you place, there is a need for a plan to place these additional products and services along the path of the consumer. It is something that needs to be so simple, yet still there, something that is within the vision path of the consumer. Many times, this creates more revenues than the main item being marketed. It is a solid part of creating multiple streams of income as well.

CHAPTER 26

LURES AND ATTRACTION MARKETING

I have a fond love of fishing, especially deep-sea fishing. It is a rush and something that gets me out of the office and into the great open waters. It is also an amazing lesson in lures and attraction. It is also a space of consumer products. Where there are needs and issues, there are solutions. These solutions are where the biggest catches are not always the fish, but the fishermen. And yes, metaphorically speaking, this applies to any area of products and consumers.

I have dropped several hundred dollars in a single bait and lure shopping experience. Even as a marketer that is always looking for the marketing and the techniques and art of it done by others, I too learn all the time.

I was in one of a few favorite locations in Newport California. There is a mystery to fishing. And it is called fishing and not catching after all. We had a guide hired to accompany us in the yacht for the next few days. He had a list of requirements for the tuna and other fish we would be targeting. It was an extensive list and like a good student I was fulfilling the list. I was enjoying myself. I mean, it is a fun experience and seeing all the gear and updated lures and devices to make you feel like you have a better chance is fun.

I was getting into one of the latest lures released. It was on the list and it was clear as you watched the other anglers coming in the store that we were clearly buying something everyone else was after as well. They were well stocked, and I was having a hard time deciding. As opposed to the many other items, these were popular and in several different colors. Not a few choices but several. Too many, to be honest. So, now I need help, because is there a difference in yellow, red, or blue? Do I need multiple colors, or is there a better one? I need an expert.

I wait patiently and go right for the owner. His son works there, and they were from the same tree (they even have the same mannerisms). After several times supporting his shop we had been conversing often. He laughed at my questions and said something that still makes me laugh to this day. I'll be sitting around; something will remind me of a fishing lure and I will chuckle hard. See, I enjoy shopping for things I am passionate about and so does anyone else. We invest in areas we care about.

He said, fish cannot see the colors. Those are to catch the fishermen. And then I lost it. I laughed so out of control. I realized that I had purchased so many different colors and lures for decades. It was hilarious. And it just proves the points of lures in both fishing lures and lures of other types attract consumers.

I found it even more funny that even as a professional marketer that understands lures and attraction marketing, I too was caught up and have been ever since I went fishing with my Grandfather four decades ago. Now as it was brought to my attention by a profiting entrepreneur, I continue to buy the flashy colors, but I laugh at myself as I do it. And it is even more entertaining when I go to a Pro Shop and watch other anglers buy into the lures.

The attraction is a large part of marketing itself. It is where we all need to pay attention and even pay attention in our own lives and how we consume. We are attracted to simple things and even not so simple. We like good looking people, and we are fascinated by the stars and celebrities.

Fishing lures catch fishermen every time and catch fish some of the time. Successful lures in marketing attract the eyeballs and bring them to the product or service being marketed. They are clever images, themes, or storylines. They are used to create a diverse marketing scheme.

Just like in fishing, the lures of a marketing campaign are used to catch the customers attention and to seep into the ascension marketing and process of interest to purchase. From cartoon characters, to celebrities, to created spokesmodels. The different campaigns are all lures to gain attention from the desired audience and customer base. These lures are used to attract the customer and potential customers that will develop over their natural course of ascension from being aware to becoming a customer.

McDonald's is really a marketing company that offers food and toys. They have lures and tie into emotions and ascension marketing extremely well. They, like Ford and Chevrolet, start with their customer acquisition at a young age. Toys. Toys are lures and used for attraction to gain the customer at a young age. The food is truly secondary. The endorphins and happiness felt by a child getting the Happy Meal with the toy inside is all it takes. Years of this process and when they are no longer children, they will see the golden arches and smile. It will tie into all sorts of happy memories and thoughts.

Businesses that understand this, usually have some experience to offer their customers that are not of age yet to be customers. Suckers and a sticker as they wait at the bank for their parents to make a deposit or pull-out cash. The incredible play set to reward them as mom and her friends share gossip over their chicken sandwiches and caesar salads. These lures and attraction marketing actions and experiences are all part of ascension marketing.

Dog friendly communities such as what is found in Napa California offer lures to keep their dog clientele happy. Dog bones to gourmet white chocolate dipped dog treats to keep their dog clientele happy and excited to bring in their owners to eat in their establishments. This is knowing and embracing their customer and the community and making it attractive for the dog whose attention and eagerness will bring in their owner more times because of it. When their best friend is happy and greeted with love it is hard to not want to come back often.

Lures and attraction marketing need to always be a tie into your marketing directions and Ascension Marketing plan. Branding itself needs to be looked at and referenced to tie in and create a loyal and connected experience ongoing with the customer. It is in the way we greet and interact with our customers as well. The little things matter. The little things are important. This is extremely important for everyone involved with the customer process as well.

CHAPTER 27

CROSS MARKETING

When you are marketing and selling multiple products, cross marketing is an absolute must. It is a natural way to add, indirectly or even straight out in addition to the main product introduction. Cross marketing allows you to reference, plant the seed of awareness about something else you offer. You have their attention and that is already a win. With cross marketing, you take their attention and feed them with the knowledge and benefits of what else you have to offer them.

If you are not offering additional or complimentary items, you are missing out on the benefits of multiple streams of income. Cross marketing and blending in additional products, services or referrals to other products and services is a major missed opportunity that could be detrimental to your income and survival within business.

It can be subtle as a reference or suggestion, or it can be a full-on introduction when they are there in your shopping cart or as they are exiting. If you are doing a write up, adding your cross over items in reference or in combination. Suggestions go a long way, as do images of the items in use together. The ideas of one with the other work. No one likes things halfway or not as good as it could be. We always want more, and we want more of the experience. So be sure to highlight the experience.

Cross marketing provides the flow for upsales and in some cases where your true profit margins are created. In the online marketing world, we refer to our upsales as bumps. We must deal with competition and solid costs for acquiring a customer. When we add in the bumps, we take a loss and turn it into break even or better. It is the ongoing cross marketing that allows the business to sustain. Without it we would have no business. This is similar to many business models. The bumps (cross marketing of other products and services) are what makes the actual business work. The bumps make it work and without it the profits to run the business do not exist. It is this very fact that created the use of cross marketing from the beginning of all business directions. Planning for it only creates more profits and more ways to succeed quicker and better overall.

It is the small things that matter. In marketing, it is never just one thing that makes it work but the combination of many things. Multiple ways, multiple understandings, and multiple methods. When done right it creates the methods for multiple streams of income.

And it is understanding of the ascension marketing along, with other marketing concepts and directions working together that makes it all work best. Some things take a while to kick in and often it is when you want to stop doing something when it finally starts to work. Marketing is never an instant solution. Again, if it were easy everyone would do it. If everyone knew how it truly worked and the time it really took to get to where it works; they would not quit. Marketing is freedom and it comes at the price of refusing to quit and to stick to it. Find a way to keep it going and understand the patience process behind it all.

Reinvest into marketing and the future is always being created. This is why an established business with clients, customers and ongoing sales is worth more. It is already undergoing success and with marketing programs in place. Acquisition is proof of a business concept. Showing that you can gain a customer and build a name and brand is valuable. Cross marketing is following those same processes but doing so smartly to gain maximum exposure to what you are offering to your customer. Sharing and expanding their understanding of what you offer in products, services and the experience is where cross marketing occurs.

It is using the same energy, expenses of marketing and customer acquisition to gain exposure to more of what you have to offer. It is also something that becomes easier and easier as you add it into your overall marketing directions.

SECTION V

RORY'S APPLIED MARKETING 101 CLASS BEGINS HERE

CHAPTER 28

CONTENT MARKETING

This is something I am extremely proud of. And something that was undervalued by my competitors and major businesses for decades. Content Marketing. This is something that only a marketer with the understanding of ascension marketing, the patience process and a true forward vision understands. It is far from instant gratification and is something you can never truly have enough of.

We live in an era where the customer does not always have the most trust in a new business or what any business says about itself. We have been made accustomed to being lied to by far too many dishonest people and businesses. This is apparent in the ways in which we make our buying decisions.

This allows for content from third parties to matter even more. And this is where content is the most powerful. It is more important today what our customers and those that experience our products and services say about us than what we do. Opinions, comments, and reviews are almost priceless. A bad review can cost you countless losses, and sadly, they are almost impossible to measure. A great review can bring in customers and help the ascension marketing processes to happen faster.

Publicizing and sharing your reviews (especially the good ones) is a vital part of the content Marketing processes. And taking the negative ones and fixing your business is a way to limit the issues. Responding to them and rectifying is always important and part of proper customer support. And if one person has a bad experience and wrote about it, you can figure they were not alone. The silent customers with a bad experience can be more devastating as you will not likely have a way to repair the spread of the damages, let alone know they existed.

The only way to build and counter the negativity is with more and more positivity and owning it. If there were problems, fix them and move forward with a new approach. Every representative of your business and process matter. This is why the new way of business will lean towards shared partnership with all that build and are part of the business success. Having the least paid person be the main interaction with the actual customer is not always wise.

Did I say not always? Let me rephrase that, it is never wise to have the least paid person have the main interaction with the customer and their experience within your business.

I have been doing content marketing even before the Internet was any form of effective communication. Direct mail, newspapers, and printed materials to support the products or services I was representing. It did not change, just became easier to do as the internet became the way of life for us all. If anything, it has become so much easier and yet most do not understand it's incredible and long-term importance.

And as more and more realize how important it is and truly how easy it can be, they will be flocking to it with ease. Remember, if it were easy everyone would be doing it.

CHAPTER 29

SOCIAL MEDIA MARKETING THROUGH THE EYES OF RORY

The social media platforms took us all by storm. Instantly we have access to platforms that we can almost reflect whatever we want as to who or what we are and stand for. In many cases, we can control the day-to-day narrative and story of whom we are, both as individuals and as a business.

I am a mass marketer. I have been building databases and marketing tools, many proprietary to my design and needs. There are companies and even other individuals that have similar or probably even far better methods and structures to do the same. We see the world as marketers. We are using this data to create more and more actions that create our wealth. So, when I tell you there is so much here in social media marketing that unsuspecting or unknowledgeable consumers do not realize, I am but scratching the surface.

There is an amazing ability today with social media marketing that, when done right, allows the marketing principles and education within these pages to really be effective. Ascension marketing, when utilized in social media marketing, is perfection. The long-term effects of sharing product placement and creation of an experience are incredible. It is affordable and duplicatable. That alone makes it powerful. And like all things that are powerful, they can be used to help or hurt your brand, business, product, or service.

This is literally power and control in how we are seen and respected by the entire world. What we post and say, and how we interact, tells our story. The truth is always going to surface. If you are posting it, it is the story of your life regardless of your desire to have it be known.

If you want to see just how many people truly do not understand marketing, just look at who and what is posted on social media. For one, social media is probably the most effective ascension marketing platform for everyday use by everyone ever created. It is free for all and creates an incredible gathering of data for use in paid marketing like never before.

The incredible ways in which it ties into artificial intelligence programming and databases for tracking, anticipating, and connecting us all with potential products, services and solutions to our shared needs is ever evolving.

No matter who you are, how you feel about marketing and sales, the very presence you have on social media is marketing and selling yourself to the world. You are building up content and utilizing ascension marketing for any that find you, follow you, or interact with your social media profiles to generate an opinion about you.

This goes for your business, your products, your services, and each and everything you represent. There is an incredible lack of understanding when anyone takes uses social media as their method of counselling, complaining, or really adding anything negative.

At the same time, we all want a positive experience. We are attracted to happiness--not misery. The laws of attraction and awareness are, if anything, amplified online. When I see people going off on their boyfriend or girlfriend, or when they express personal issues of any kind, it is self-evident that they want to have the most expensive form of counselling ever. So expensive, that they do not realize it. Anything negative will attract negative.

The law of attraction states that what we put out we attract. If we are positive and outgoing, we will attract others of the same. When you use any communication platform, what you put out, you are sure to attract. Be careful what you ask for.

The law of awareness states that once we are aware of a product or service, we will now be aware of it. My favorite story about the law of awareness is when I was in my early 20's. I was so excited about the new Mazda Miata. I wanted a black one. That next Saturday, I went to a lot and drove one off the lot. I was attracted to it as a new car that I believed no one else had. Now, owning one and being fully aware of them, from the moment I left the car lot all I saw was another Mazda Miata everywhere.

Frustrations shared never give you a reward worth the costs. If you have issues with anything be ready to own it and the costs that come with it. Because, forever anyone watching, looking into you, or associated and connected to you in any way can now take and use that information to conclude anything about you. Jobs and career options as well as long term opinions are now affected by your shared life online.

Once you make your followers aware of how you are, they are aware of it. And now, it will only grow in awareness for them. Good, bad, dramatic, or uplifting, all of it your choice.

There is only so much time and so many things that you can influence or control. The send button, the post button and the comment buttons are all marketing weapons for the good or bad of your presence online. Use them wisely and know that what goes online stays online. History is being created. Patterns are constantly being formed and tracked. Your buying habits and responses are forming marketing advantages for your life today, tomorrow, and far into the future.

With all of this is one constant. Using social media marketing is so valuable it is an absolute must. It is also an absolute must that you do it with the exact message and direction you want to put yourself, your business, your product, your service out to the world with. Negative is multiplied and positive is forever needing to be reinforced.

Once you start the process of Social Media Marketing, do not let off or quit. It is a forever process that needs to continue. It is also important that you utilize every social media platform. Be ready for change and shifts. There are no gains to only work on one. What is hot and trending today is today. Tomorrow something else may be trendier. Do not get married to one. Be ready for innovation, change and be ready to adapt.

At the same time, it is not the end-all be-all. It is a part of your marketing tools. Not the only one. Multiple streams of income are connected with multiple methods of marketing. There is a reason radio, television, print, billboards, signs, emails, SMS, text and so many other forms of communication are still in use by the largest of companies. Nothing is the end all be all of marketing platforms. We truly can never market enough. Coca-Cola, McDonald's and even home and auto insurance rely on every possible marketing platform they can to keep relevant to the consumer.

CHAPTER 30

LINK POSTING, ONLINE ADS AND THE POWER OF NUMBERS

When I discovered the internet, and the ways of marketing were made available, I was hungry to try everything. My marketing world before the internet was made possible by direct mail marketing. There was no internet with consumers and potential clients to reach out too.

There were mailing lists, the post office, and the ability to pay per piece to be printed and postmarked to everyone you wanted to reach out as well. So, you had to be good at your game, or you would lose out big time. Hard cash. It was something that may not pan out initially. It took time to get to people, and time for them to respond.

One ad may not do anything, but hundreds of ads placed throughout the country would get more and more responses over time. Purchasing multiple days of ad placements, and even multiple weeks or months, would prove out to be effective overall, or a giant waste of money. It had its ups, and its downs. Though the economics were, and still are, different, the one thing that remained consistent was that more is more. There was seemingly no saturation point in posting ads.

So, when the internet became an option, things were instantly less risky. There were quick delivery and response times, and postage was traded for ad space costs, or, in many cases, no cost or next-to-nothing as online locations were building up. Still to this day, more is more. Only now, there are huge differences in paid and free advertising.

It is all relative. The methods of online marketing can help the individual or family to create income streams so they can have an incredible life. It is having the right systems, training, and knowledge, and then applying it to the right products and services. It is understanding the art of it in a way that the product, service, or combination of products and services can be interchanged.

The process and systems are where the strength and speed of gaining time and financial freedoms through marketing are realized.

CHAPTER 31

THREE-LEGGED MARKETING TABLE

All my life, I have been studying the cunning of men. I have watched and researched the ins and outs of marketing, and then tried many methods. All to where I worked to understand the decision-making processes of why and what motivated the buyer to buy.

I have seen some incredible things in marketing success. In doing so, I have broken things down into simplistic formats based on what is happening to make the success happen. In marketing, it is the use of a minimum of three legs to a marketing table. This is a minimum, any and all marketing campaigns need at least three to be successful.

I have always explained it as a marketing table. It is where you can sit down and watch your marketing efforts take shape. Like any table, it needs at least three legs to be standing. One leg, and it has nothing to balance with; two legs, and it can only falter and fall; however, adding a third leg, or more, allows you to stabilize the marketing table.

Anything I take on as a marketing project requires that I have three legs to the marketing table that will be set up and used for the project. I never start with one thing, but always three. When I do this, my success is almost guaranteed. Depending on budgets and time, things can work out to a plan, or even an expectation.

When I initially began teaching my RRR247 structure, we had three solid legs of marketing. The other legs had to be built on later. As the income came in from the proven programs we marketed—each with the same three legs of the marketing table to build them—we reinvested and created the fourth leg, then the fifth Leg. Today, we have over nine legs of marketing, and success is building constantly.

RRR247 is based upon a core marketing structure that we call performance blogging. I developed, created, and established this in 2008. It was an evolution of marketing starting in 1989, and it progressed through direct mail, magazine ads, newspaper, and then pushed into the online world where it continues evolving. It is a form of absolute marketing tables for anything that is added.

The initial three legs to the marketing table that we begin teaching our students within RRR247 include:

- **Content Marketing.** This is then used for search engine optimization, and it connects with the other marketing Legs.
- **Link Posting of Ads**. These are targeted ads that go to the specific content pages created for each and every product or service being marketed.
- **Social Media Marketing.** We do this with proven steps, methods, and processes to engage and attract customers.

These are incredible as they are available for every student we train. From here, the knowledge and training make the additional legs of marketing even more successful. Then, we go into an additional five legs of marketing. The correct use and utilization of all nine legs of marketing allow for success. Only quitting can create defeat.

Today, more than ever, success is possible in marketing. For me, it is the creation of the social media platforms that gave us a third leg, and that is when success for all that followed our training and applications became more of a reality. It goes to three legs of the marketing table, the minimum to seeing things through to success. The odds are greater with a stable table of at least three legs.

With my clients, they would come to me to build up their marketing. They would have print ads going out in some cases, or even billboards. In my explanation, they would have only one, or two, marketing legs. They would be missing one or two legs needed for stability. They would be coming to me because they needed help. They were spending money, and, in most cases, they were concentrating on one marketing method only.

Ascension marketing is real, and the more legs to the marketing table you have, the more you are allowing ascension marketing to occur. We cannot measure the success of marketing in a true measurement because it takes time. Sure, in paid for social media campaigns, we have access to great analytics for the "now" responses, and purchases, even, but it does not let you see the global perspective that could be taking years, decades, and more. This is where timeliness and sticking around pays off. Those who stick around get paid and sticking around and being there is 90% of success. Trust in the systems. Trust in the marketing. Then follow and buy into the patient process of ascension marketing. Stick around and do not quit.

This is in perspective to your efforts as well. Having the legs of marketing and using them is hand in hand with success. If you take the gas off, the ascension marketing loses its effectiveness. McDonald's and Coca-Cola do not stop marketing. They know that it is a long-time process and today helps today and into the future. If you want to see success, you never take the gas off Marketing. It makes the World go around.

Pressing the support to my three-legged marketing table, we can look at all sorts of successful businesses. The more they can be in front of you, the more methods or legs of their marketing table, and the more direction, the better. Geico, Progressive, Allstate, and about every other insurance company have multiple legs to their marketing tables. Geico will hit the consumer with several different lures and angles. The Geico gecko, celebrity tie-ins and their themes of how easy Geico is compared to some impossible things happening within the commercial. They have the caveman, and all of it based on how easy it is with them. Sounds a lot like the "if it was easy everyone would be doing it" understanding. Crazy, right?

Same for Progressive, Allstate and the other insurance companies. Using multiple characters, lures, and themes to grab your attention. These are not by accident or for fun. They are well advised marketing directions that are running on at least three different legs of their marketing table. They have separate themes and while I only gave you a few examples, now as you watch companies with incredible success and how they market, you will be aware of it and learn and gain from it.

The perspective of most everyone I start to teach and instruct comes from consumer understanding. When you can open up and see the marketing angles, you will be aware of the marketing concepts, and processes that are in play. Marketing is incredible and it is more complex. The trick is again, "If it were easy, everyone would be doing it." The more you understand and see it, the easier it will be for you to understand. The more you understand the more you can apply it to your legs of marketing for whatever you are working on.

Have fun, and if you are running multiple marketing legs, you can worry less about one not working as well as you would like. Diversify your marketing risk. All of it connects to the ascension marketing and the patient process of it all.

SECTION VI

THE GLOBAL VISION. MAKING THE WORLD AMAZING.

CHAPTER 32

THE NEW WAY OF WORKING TOGETHER

There is an incredible opportunity that is happening in our lifetime. Right here, right now. It is a change in how we can work together in the open marketplace, local, and global. As the world has been evolving digitally, so have the available methods of communication and sharing of information.

As we wipe away jobs and processes, we also create new processes, and new jobs, and solutions as needed.

Communications evolved from one on one to literally thousands at one time. Add in social Media and now millions communicate at once. Sharing ideas, ideologies, and more, now happens within seconds versus days, months, or years.

Methods to learn and gain from the education out there are becoming faster and faster. There are more new methods created than ever before. It is our inability to adapt and learn that limits us. We are working together, growing together and literally changing the world together.

All forms of marketing and systems require human interaction and emotional support for the client experience at some level. This creates shared opportunities for more and more people as we grow.

Those who can create marketing systems and client experiences that are attractive to the client, will only need to add more partners to grow their marketplace. The future is for those that adapt and change the labor of time to be focused on the client experience. All other areas of the business can, and should, be automated by technology.

The largest of companies in any category will grow with a combined experience and way of sharing the wealth created by marketing being done properly to make sales order taking. Then, the ongoing support of the client experience by the partners sharing the success of the overall process.

CHAPTER 33

CORE VALUES

When you are building anything up correctly, you need a solid path on how you are going to get there. It takes a measurement and a quality that you must adhere to, to keep order and stay organized by. These are your core values as a person, as a family unit, as a business and as an organization. It is the governing laws to which you will abide by and expect those you are working with to abide by. For our business, we run under three core values. Created after decades of business ownership, employing hundreds of employees over the decades, and seeing the exact environment we were wanting to be a part of. We set the boundaries and keep it as the focus to how we do things.

This is how we lead and work with our Instructors within our RRR247 Platform to teach and enable others to gain freedom in time and wealth through marketing.

We Love Everyone

We operate for success with set protocols in training for our students. We utilize time management to teach, inspire, and support the successes of our students. Always.

We Are A Family

We help each other, always. Each instructor is expected to guide and help any and all students.

Strive For Awesome-Ness

In everything we do, in every way. Always.

We keep our core values simple, but it is all about how we want things done. It ties into our key golden rules and it is never about chasing the money. It is about building up and supporting the people. The people are everything. Building up, training, supporting and being there along the way as they grow and achieve is really what this is all about and always needs to be about.

CHAPTER 34

APPLYING CORE VALUES IN EVERYDAY LIFE

The core values are those that fit all aspects of how you want your direction of your habits, processes, and work to go. Your core values should be universal in how they work and allow things to flow. In your business and in your home, it should relate to how you interact with others without the difference of the workplace environment. The best core values transcend and become a part of our DNA. If the core values are not those you would utilize in your home with your family and friends, you may want to rethink or modify them.

The more they can be based on the ways and manners of the golden rules, the better they will work and become part of your habits for success. If it is something you would have govern you and your actions; then it is most likely a good fit for those you will be working with, living with, and growing in all things good here on earth.

We all thrive when in a healthy and happy environment. There are always plenty of life issues to give any of us a bad day on any given day. Find a way to make involvement with you and your marketing, a happy and safe place, and the universe will reward you.

CHAPTER 35

APPLYING CORE VALUES IN BUILDING AN ONLINE MARKETING COMMUNITY

When you are building an online community, it is especially important to keep and adhere to your core values. Once you establish your core values, and how you are going to function, and the rules you will be functioning with, you need to stick to them. This is especially the case with an online marketing community. It is hard to build, and as it becomes easy, and more and more join and become a part of it, you will need to protect it.

Short-sighted persons with lacking integrity may look to create issues. These will range from causing drama and creating time-sucking issues. One bad apple can indeed spoil the entire basket.

Do not be afraid to fire or remove a bad apple from your community. The way you treat bad apples says a lot about you and your online marketing community. When bad apples are left to be bad apples, you will lose the respect of the good apples.

Law and order are welcomed by all that want a long term solution. You will also find that the bad apples will cause more wasted time than they can ever be worth. And the ripple effects of their wasted time and drama are not worth your time. Eliminating it will only make room for more success.

I cannot personally share how incredible this aspect has impacted my entire life. It is also a reason why we attract the right people into our community. We have choices in life, including what we do to build income streams and whom we work with. We are attracted to likeminded people and likeminded directions that those people are looking to go.

As a mentor, I strive to be at my peak awesomeness every day. I am proud to be giving back and know that I am there to pay it forward. The more I give of myself to truly help others, in following the core values, the more it is rewarded back to me.

These core values connected me with incredible mentors, partners, and shared visionaries, to help make the world a truly better place. There is a circular path that we are all on. This path allows us to connect again with people we meet and interact with along the way. Living by the golden rules and following core values you can set yourself up to gain amazing things with the help of others as your circular paths cross.

When my Grandfather told me my word was everything, he was 100% correct. I have been raised to give everything my all, my best. To do things the right way. No shortcuts. But primarily to do what I say I will do. Always. My Grandfather told me that if I did what I said I would do; I would stand out. Honor your word and you will shine. It is that simple. And he was right.

This path has connected me with incredible people. Many of which are in business with me and are part of the incredible things we are doing to help others. They are of similar Core Values and come from an incredible place of helping and serving others all the time.

CHAPTER 36

END WITH A NEVER-ENDING PATH. AN INTRODUCTION TO THE PERFORMANCE BLOGGING SYSTEM (PBS).

This book started out as a way for me to leave a Legacy of Information into print, archive, and to share with the world. I truly hope that you have gained in some knowledge and insight to better your life and more importantly, the lives of others. There is a lot of understanding of your customer, client, and human beings, that can be learned and understood best from the eyes of a marketer. As the months of working on this book transpired it became more and more a resource to share with both my students and for anyone looking to gain from the decades of applied marketing, I have been blessed with all these years. And as a human being that loves others, I know it is my duty to share this knowledge and path to time and financial freedoms.

I trust that anyone that reads these pages of shared knowledge will gain from it. I ask that you pay it forward and share the knowledge. This is a way to grow the ability for more and more people to share in the gains of commerce and ecommerce. This is vital knowledge. A gift that can work today and into our generations to come. Enjoy the mystique and magic that is marketing. Understanding it and applying it is one thing but celebrating the results and fun of it is where it is truly worthwhile.

I have been able to take the teachings and understandings as shared within these pages and applied them to a process, a system that I created called the Performance Blogging System. It is not just about an online presence by which all the teachings and applied teachings are supported and proven out every day, but it is a truly special and complete environment for success. It is a platform that not only works to create multiple streams of income, but it allows the teaching and results of all the Marketing training within these pages to be explained and seen.

It is the same principles and Marketing Understanding that allow incredible things to happen for large corporations; that when applied through a system backed by the training and understanding of my life's work that can create a truly special thing. A way to truly help the family. A family that runs like a profitable business can endure, enjoy, and grow. It is not just the incomes that can be created to allow for better everything, but the understanding and applied happiness available through full understanding. To give and support the dreams, goals, and needs of others is to be of purpose. Not for one's own gains, but for the gains of others to which you gain blessings beyond.

Giving the family the gift of time together and the means to enjoy life. The ability to travel and enjoy this World. Not just the corner of it you were born into, but the glorious Abundances of the earth as provided by our God, the maker of everything.

Should you or anyone you know need a system and an environment to which you can be supported, loved and successful, you need only look us up. We are applied users of the very methods, knowledge, and truths of what you just read and took in.

If you are building your passion and progressing, then please be sure to pass on success and knowledge to those you come across. See to me, the sharing of knowledge is like sharing an Amazing Bottle of Wine. To celebrate the Freedom that is created through the eyes, understanding and application of Marketing, check out the incredible Freedom Chardonnay. A true fine wine, like Freedom is the absolute of Taste and what is Meant to be ours. It is incredible and you thoroughly enjoy it. But to share the enjoyment and the pleasure it brings you with another; that is the fullest of the enjoyment. Here is to wine, freedom and the sharing and gifts it brings to all those we share them with.

With love and support for your best life ever,

Rory Edison Ricord

CHAPTER 37

AN ENCORE OF GRATITUDE

This entire experience of creating this book has really allowed me to reflect and be so thankful. I have to end this book with a comment about some key persons that have allowed me to be me and to fly. Sometimes the student is an incredible teacher. Sometimes the mentor is always there at the right times. Sometimes there are key moments or happenstances that occur that set your path up in incredible ways. The universe works in incredible ways and God is great. We all deserve to have the overabundance available in all aspects of our life and as I figured out life, I have also put those findings down in this book. The pages are here and for me it has always been through the eyes of a Marketer and Marketing has truly led me to time and financial freedom. To see it reflected and be shared by those that listen and use this shared information is without words to explain, but it is truly happiness to pull on.

So, I thank you for reading and trust you will apply all you can, as you can. God Bless.

SPECIAL THANKS

To my wife and partner Tanya Ricord. Who is so much more a guide to keep me on path and to balance out my life with our incredible family. She is a true "American Wife" that is at the business tables with me and has the counselling and guidance that truly make me look far more incredible than I deserve.

To all the instructors with RRR247 that are sharing the vision and are paying it forward 24-7 as we change the environment and adhere to our core values always.

To the two Richards in my life that guided me in ways that set me up for the incredible things to come in my later years. Richard Merlin Thorup (Grandpa, I miss you and work to make you proud every day) and Richard Davidson who impacted me far more than he will ever know.

And to the Man that helped me with so much, including the final touches that always take the longest. Kosta Gara, to whom thank you will never be enough.

Additional thanks to some incredible people that through happenstances and circular paths, some incredible things are happening, and I am certain will continue even further.

Scott Fabian, John Shaver and David Maggard who have been incredible marketing partners and to who's keen abilities and strife for perfection in the online marketing arena has been monumental.

Peter Bradford, from competition to best friend. It is always enjoyable as we navigate in business and shared vision, creation, and innovation in this marketing world we see. Your wife Heather is great too.

James Borzilleri, the incredible decades of your friendship and business counsel has been incredible all these years. Your true friendship is unmeasurable. The times we share on Yachts and incredible adventures while planning our next moves in business have been priceless. Thank you.

Nile Eddy, to whom I have always bonded with as a brother. Through it all, thick and thin, you are a rock. Deep sea fishing is always incredible with you.

Daniel and Sarah Goncalves out in Sydney Australia, who have been connected to Tanya and I for an incredible lifetime now. Your uniqueness and shared vision and understanding has been instrumental in our path. Thank you.

Brett Hudson, to which an incredible happenstance in Aruba set a course for partnership in making the world better through wine and so much more. Never underestimate the power of connecting with likeminded people.

Anthony Powell, to whose circular path crossed mine multiple times and whose incredible work ethic has been an inspiration for decades.

Peter Antoniou, who has been instrumental in tasting skills, programming skills (beyond) and truly incredible to create systems to carry things into tomorrow with. The wine and food experiences we share as often as possible are far too enjoyable.

Jim Franckowiak, friend, attorney, and business partner. Decades of growth and understanding. The path has been awesome my friend. Huge thanks for the years of making sure we always do things right.

To the incredible and fortunate lives all in circular paths that I have shared over the past decades and to those that are in route to connect in my future, these blessings are incredible.

Thank you.